A Party of One
Volume 1

By Margo Oxendine

*For Mary,
Enjoy!
Margo Oxendine*

Snowy Mountain Publishing, Inc.
Monterey, Virginia

First Edition, March 2013
Snowy Mountain Publishing, Inc.
Monterey, Virginia

Copyright© 2013 by Margo Oxendine.
All rights reserved under International and Pan-American Copyright Conventions.
Published in the United States by Snowy Mountain Publishing, Inc.
/DBA/ The Recorder, www.TheRecorderOnline.com.
ISBN: 978-0-9887929-0-6

Cover illustration by Joe McLain.

Acknowledgements

For years now, I have yammered about the "four or five" books I have languishing inside my computer. But I, the quintessential procrastinator, never quite found the time to get to the task of putting them together.

I've always been an optimist; one who strives to get through an adversity by turning it into an advantage. And I've been lucky at that … so far.

So what it took was an adversity – losing one writing job – to spur me into action. I combed through almost 800 columns I've written over the past 12 years, and culled the 65 you'll find here. They're some of my favorites, and I hope you like them, too.

None of this would have been possible, though, without the great newspaper and magazine people who took a chance that my oft-offbeat ramblings might interest at least some of their readers.

So, big thanks to Horton Beirne of the Virginian-Review newspaper in Covington, who helped me to turn another adversity into the advantage of a weekly column in his paper, "Life … You Gotta Love It!"

And I will never forget, or have enough gratitude for, Richard Johnstone and Bill Sherrod of Cooperative Living, who showed up out of the blue, took me to lunch (they know how to get to a girl!), and suggested I write a column for their magazine. We called it "Rural Living," and I wrote it as the experiences of a city girl now living the country life.

And then, there's the incomparable Anne Adams, publisher of The Recorder newspaper in Highland County. One of my dearest friends turned out to be one of my best bosses ever; I consider myself oh, so lucky. It was Anne who encouraged me to get this book into production, and she who cleared all the paths that seemed somewhat insurmountable to a procrastinating technopeasant. Thank you, Anne, from the bottom of my heart!

These acknowledgements wouldn't be complete without mention of another great friend, Suzanne Osborne. My gosh, but that woman is a powerhouse. I don't think there is a time in the past five years that, when we've gotten together, she hasn't nagged me to get off my duff and put this book on the page. Thanks, Suzanne; you're an exceptional encourager. I no longer need feel like a guilty slacker when we go out to dinner!

Table of Contents

Of Knives and Pantyhose 1
Dominus Vobiscum 3
My Parochial Revenge 5
We're on the Right Road! 7
Daddy Grabs a Bomb 9
Daddy's Parting Gift 11
Just a Little Fire 13
Flying Miss Daisy 15
Babies, Boomer and Rutabaga, Too! 17
Of Pasta and Panic 19
An Alarming Trip to the City 21
Ask Auntie Margo 23
Revenge of the Critters 25
The Critters Have their Say 27
The Dreaded Drone of Danger 29
No Bother at All 31
Snooping with Dogs 33
Like Cats and Dogs 35
A Toddler in the House 37
I Encounter a Viscious Beast 39
Max's Curious Adventure 41
Swimming with the Fishes 43
Dallying with the Dolphins 45
Wherein I Ride an Elephant 47
Say Hay! 49
Bee Very Afraid 51
Regrets: I Have a Few 53
Whistle While You Work 55
A Letter from my Contractor 57
Selling Country Property 59
The Mystery of the Missing Nuggets 61
I Learn to Play Ball 63
Jailbirds 65
'Those Were the Days, My Friend' 67
The Mishappetizer 69
I'm a Stranger Here 71

Table of Contents

A Yacht in the Aegean 73
Something in Common After All 75
I Venture to Havana 77
June: National Rural Laundry Month 79
The Kinky Burglar 81
I am Handy! 83
In Praise of Pillows 85
My Favorite Sentence 87
Love a Teacher 89
Shattered Expectations 91
Somebody Laves Me 93
An Unhappy Camper 95
I Love to Snovel Show! 97
The Pokey Dokes 99
The Rural Wave 101
Dancing the Dance 103
On the Rivah 105
The Surprise Wedding 107
I Learn New Tricks 109
The Party Dog 111
Patron Saints to Know and Love 113
My Thanksgiving Feast 115
The Joy of Meals on Wheels 117
Christmas Spirit: A Special Delivery 119
An Exciting Trip to the Dump 121
The Big Ugly 123
My Lucky Day 125
The Turtle Takes the Prize 127
Two Empty Chairs 129

Introduction

The secret to writing, it is said, is this: Write what you know. Culling through columns for this book, I discovered my life is about family, animals, travel, food and adventure. Lucky me!

My writing career began one morning in Key West. I was aboard a Spanish galleon tour boat, working for the famous treasure hunter, Mel Fisher.

A barefoot fellow swaggered aboard, wearing a red bikini. Two ammo belts crisscrossed his chest. He carried a rifle. He chomped on a cigar.

That swashbuckler was Bob Marx, a rival but friendly treasure hunter. He was also the adventure editor of Argosy, a popular men's magazine at the time. He was looking for someone to write Mel's life story, and he decided that someone was I.

And so it began, some 35 years ago.

I always dreamed of being a writer but, when it came time to go to college, my father refused to pay for me to "become a damn reporter." This is how most law enforcement officials feel about those in the journalism profession.

By golly, I showed him. I majored in theater. We all know how that turned out.

While in Key West, I became part of a comedy troupe, "Vital Signs." I wrote some skits, and performed in even more. My fondest memory is the night I was doing one of my shticks and noticed, in the front row of the Waterfront Theater, this foursome: Tennessee Williams, Eartha Kitt, Truman Capote and Shel Silverstein. They were laughing out loud. Eartha was slapping her knees. I decided I'd head to San Francisco and pursue stand-up comedy as a career. We all know how that turned out.

I have been paid to sit somewhere and write about things for decades. I began by freelancing for magazines, then wrote comedy, and then became a newspaper reporter. I was pretty good at it. But I got tired of "poking through people's purses" and struggling to appear alert and interested at local government meetings.

So, I veered off and became a museum curator. Loved it. Discovered that maybe I should have majored in history, after all.

But the lure of journalism beckoned. I began to write columns for The Virginian-Review newspaper in Covington, and Cooperative Living magazine. Then, after one fateful call one day, I was back at The Recorder — the best weekly newspaper in Virginia, if not the whole country.

Now, people pay me to sit around at home in pajamas or sweatpants and write about life. You gotta love it!

Here's how the title "A Party of One" came about. In California, I was a licensing agent for the music-copyright entity ASCAP. My territory included all of California from Sacramento north, and all of Nevada except for Las Vegas.

My weeks were spent driving around, looking for entertainment. This might have been fun, except that, once I found entertainment in a bar or casino or restaurant, I had to convince the owners that they owed money for something they thought they had already paid for. I won't waste too many words, but just because you've paid the band doesn't mean you've paid the copyright owners their share of the pie.

One day, the boss issued me a tall task: licensing all the brothels in Nevada.

Thus it was that I found myself one evening checking into the Mizpah Hotel in Tonopah. (Note to single ladies looking for love: Get yourselves to Tonopah; the town is teeming with good looking, lonely men!) I was in Tonopah to license "Bobby's Buckeye Bar," a brothel described in a published guide to such establishments as "a long, pink structure on a rise." Enough said.

So, I'm in line to be seated in the Mizpah Hotel dining room.

"How many in your party?" the hostess asks.

"I'm a party of one," I proclaim.

Five well-dressed cattlemen behind me overheard the exchange.

"Well, little lady," one said, tipping his Stetson, "that's about the saddest thing I ever heard. You're joining us."

I barely remember the fun dinner of lobster and steak, but I've never forgotten that this was the night I learned what I was born to be: A Party of One.

Welcome to my party!

Little Margo as she imagines herself ...   ... and, like the Wizard of Oz, as she really is.

Margo and her sister, Kathy McCollum, enjoy some dress-up time, wherein young Margo indulges in her ambition to be a "dance hall girl."

Margo in her heyday: Key West, Florida, July 1978.

David McCollum Jr. and his wife, Dorothy McCollum, in his Chief of Security office at The Homestead hotel in Hot Springs, Va.

David McCollum Sr. (holding hammer), clowns around, unbeknownst to his wife Gertrude, right, and her sister, Jenny, at the family's Myrtle Beach, CT cottage, the "Gertrude Mae."

Foreword

By Richard G. Johnstone Jr.

Writing a foreword is the literary equivalent of serving as a warm-up comedian, or an opening band. You're flattered to be asked, of course, but what the audience, the crowd, the reader really wants is the headliner. Now.

So, if done correctly, a foreword should illuminate the author, be good in its quality (leaving great to the author's work that follows), and perhaps most importantly, be brief. I believe I'm up to this task: I've known Margo for more than a decade, primarily as one of her editors. Check. My writing would clearly pale alongside, but may appear serviceable when merely preceding, Margo's. Check. Now as to being brief…

On occasion, some have suggested that my essays in Cooperative Living magazine are overly long, populated with sentences that make clear why. In the instance of this warm-up routine for Margo, though, I intend to prove them wrong. (Oops, just wasted 16 words refuting a reputation for verbosity. Drat, add 10 more to the count from the preceding sentence. Now 11 more. Now three. Two. One.)

When you think about it, Bath County is a small town composed of many villages, so most of you already know Margo, as a neighbor or friend. And the thousands of readers who faithfully follow her through her essays in The Recorder and Cooperative Living feel as if they know her.

And that's because her essays have the texture and tone of stories shared by a close friend. A friend who mixes zesty prose and lyrical language to paint a richly rounded portrait of her life experiences, from the mundane to the magical, the nostalgic to the nonsensical. Her stories are tethered to the home place of Bath County that she loves and where she grew up, of course, but many also recount her earlier ports-of-call in Key West and San Francisco, where she lived as a young stand-up comedian and budding writer, in the process gaining a broader world view.

And yet, disproving Thomas Wolfe, Margo showed that you really can go home again, if not to Asheville, then to Ashwood. And to Bolar and Bacova, Hot and Warm Springs, Millboro and Mitchelltown, and Mountain Grove too. When the mountains called, Margo's heart listened. And her always-elegant shoes led her home.

And thank goodness for the rest of us that she returned. Her stories enrich us: they're life-affirming, bright and brassy, and as honest as a child's prayer. With Margo's background in stand-up comedy, and the laughs she evokes with her columns, most folks probably think of her as a comedy writer. I think of her, though, as a superb writer who's also funny. Her columns are usually VERY funny, in fact, but in an organic way, as a natural outgrowth of her stories, not as their point. Margo doesn't dispense punch lines; she dispenses lines with punch.

When you're reading a Margo Oxendine column, you feel you're there with her, on her beloved porch, screened of course! (As she wrote in one of her columns, "My porch is a wonderland….We are in; bugs are out.") On the comfy porch of her columns, she shares her life stories, always with a smile, sometimes with a wince or a grimace, occasionally with a groan, but never, ever with venom.

When you think about it, through all of her travels and triumphs, health scares and hallelujah moments, her life has become part of ours. For this greatest gift, Margo, we offer our thanks.

And so, without further delay, it's my privilege to turn the stage, er, these pages, over to that Muse of the Mountains, that Poet of the Porch, that Connoisseur of Coffee and Cold Weather, that Lover of Low Tech, that Storyteller with Heart AND Soul, ladies and gentlemen, we now present Bath County's Ambassador to All, our witty friend and wonderful neighbor, the one, the only … Margo!

A frequent visitor to Bath and Highland counties, Richard Johnstone is the longtime executive editor of Cooperative Living magazine, in which Margo's column "Rural Living" has appeared since 2000. The Richmond-based magazine is published for the 500,000 customer-owners of Virginia's 13 local electric cooperative utilities.

Of Knives and Pantyhose

How did you ring in the New Year?

I departed from my usual cocktail-pajamas-slippers-Leno fest in my club chair. In fact, I had two places to go.

Ah, the life of a Hot Springs party girl.

This was indeed a most gala holiday party season. Every single event was fun and fabulous, glittery and glamorous.

The hectic hoopla actually became – dare I say? – rather routine. Decide on a festive outfit, bathe, primp, plaster on the pantyhose, don a pair of new purple pumps, hop in the car.

It finally got to the point where, instead of attending live musical theater at The Homestead last Tuesday, I opted for the quiet solitude of my comfy chair.

I know that, by the time March rolls around, I'll regret that. Great parties seem to come in a glorious glut. Then they disappear altogether.

At one gathering last week, a dog ate my shoes. Well, one shoe, actually. Still, when one navy silk evening pump with tassels and glittery adornments dies, its mate is of little use.

I was dangling my shoe underneath the dinner table, and soon decided to chuck the footwear. It felt good, secretly rubbing my stockinged feet on the carpet. Besides, how were the other nine diners to know?

When I tried to put them back on, one shoe was missing. I danced my foot around under the table, but couldn't find it.

Moments later, our hostess holds aloft my pump.

"Is this anyone's?" she inquired.

Red-faced, I watched as the other diners passed my shoe toward me, much as if I'd asked for the potatoes. A half-moon piece of the heel was missing. And there, nestled inside, was a glob of food Penny the Terrier had apparently found distasteful.

This week, I received a mysterious package from Talbot's. Inside was a new pair of navy suede flats, with a gift card from Penny. All I can tell you is, that dog has taste.

I began New Year's Eve at Garth Newel Music Center in Warm Springs. It was quite the special occasion; the first time I'd been to that event, but certainly not the last.

Everything was wonderful, save for one misfortune: a delicate operation involving pantyhose. And a table knife.

As I'd left the house that evening, my pantyhose developed a big snag that did not bode well. For insurance, I put a backup pair in a plastic bag, and tossed it in the car.

Sure enough, minutes after arriving, my pantyhose went kerflooey. During the concert, I could feel them disintegrating. Just before dinner began, I raced out to the car and grabbed the plastic bag of backup stockings.

I was congratulating myself on this foresight when I realized that, in order to complete the switch, I'd have to take off my new shoes. And I'd need a shoehorn to get them back on. I pondered this on the way back inside, and hit upon the perfect make-do shoehorn: my table knife.

I skulked to the ladies' room, the knife and plastic bag hidden in the folds of my skirt. I entered the middle of three stalls and set to work. The knife clinked against the porcelain tank cover. The plastic bag rustled as I removed the stockings. Other than these sounds, the ladies' room was silent.

I made the usual grunts and groans of a woman pressing herself into pantyhose. And I couldn't help giggling.

Mission complete, I exited the stall. Imagine my surprise to find the room full of ladies, all intently eyeing me. You could read their thoughts: "What in heaven's name has she been doing in there?"

I made a show of walking to the wastebasket, and depositing the plastic baggie of dead stockings.

"Pantyhose explosion," I explained.

They all nodded knowingly, and laughed.

Thankfully, no one asked me to explain the knife.

— January 2004

Dominus Vobiscum

Despite my griping when I hear the alarm at 5:30 Sunday mornings – the only morning it is necessary – I have come to realize that I really like going to church. Surprisingly, it is often the high point of my week.

This was not always so.

It all started about age two. Mom and Daddy and I would drive to church. Mom would dutifully go inside. Daddy and I would sit in the car and wait. He would read the funny papers to me.

Daddy was a state trooper, and gone for most of my waking hours every day. The reading of the funny papers – just the two of us – was our special time. I was always a little disappointed to see Mom streaming out the door with the other Catholics. Daddy always cracked a joke about how Catholics were quite pious in church, but once they got into the parking lot, things changed dramatically. That was before he, too, became a Catholic. Then he, too, became as hell-bent as the rest of them to get back on the road.

When I was about four, Mom decided it was time I should be going to church. It was rather exciting that first day – I always wondered just what went on in there while we were laughing over the comics.

Once was enough. There was a lot of sitting and standing and kneeling. Everything was in a strange language I could not understand. After I inspected the hats each lady absolutely had to wear – and this was another thing: I detested that silly hat on my head – after I had made eye contact or stuck out my tongue at the other fidgety children, I'd had quite enough.

To top it off, I had to be quiet. I was not supposed to whisper, or ask questions, or giggle or, above all, sigh loudly with sheer boredom.

Today's children are smarter than we were. They are well versed in the bathroom game. As soon as they get bored, I see them tugging at the appropriate parent's sleeve. And quickly off they go. At our church, this means they must first go outside, where the birds are singing and the sun is shining and the flowers are grinning. Funny, but on rainy or bitter-cold days, very few children need to be taken to the bathroom.

Things were different back in my day. If you had to go to the bathroom, that was just tough. "Hold it," Mom would mutter, and that was that. Another ploy foiled.

The second Sunday I was expected to attend church, I hatched a devious plan. By that time I was dressing myself. I remember this like it was yesterday. I buttoned a frilly white blouse over my little plaid skirt, then some socks, and those cursed brown oxfords I was forced to wear. I chuckled to myself at the brilliance of my plan.

I rode quietly to church in the backseat. As Mom and I got out I looked back, and saw Daddy gathering the Sunday newspaper to read. I smiled to myself.

Once in church, I sat quietly. I did not want to reveal my secret too early. Things got off to their usual lugubrious start – the standing, the kneeling, the Latin. When I was certain it was too late for Mom to decide we had to turn around and run back home, I tugged on her sleeve.

"What is it?" she hissed.

In as loud a whisper as I could muster, I delivered the news: "I forgot my underpants!"

She checked and, sure enough, there I was, peeking out for all to see. I was hustled back to the car, where I enjoyed the funny papers. From that day on, though, I always had to pass inspection on Sunday mornings.

— May 2010

My Parochial Revenge

I was an over-achiever in school, even from first grade.

My mother taught me to read and write by the time I was three years old. Perhaps that had something to do with it.

I was in first grade at St. Louis Catholic School in Alexandria. There were sixty of us in our class. Sister Paula Francis was our teacher. She was a stern taskmaster; no-nonsense; immaculate in her dress and demeanor.

Sister would ask us lots of questions. We were to raise our hands if we knew the answer.

I always knew the answer. But Sister did not call on me often enough, in my opinion.

She would call on other children, many of whom did not know the answer. I would sit there at my desk, my hand raised high in the air. A sense of urgency would overtake me, as child after child was called upon to answer – everyone, it seemed, except me.

Before long, I'd be sitting there, waving wildly. I vividly recall my most frantic wave: Touch my head with my hand, then swing it down and touch the floor, then, pop back up and touch my head again.

How could Sister ignore me? I'd wonder. I know the answer!

Finally, in desperation, I'd shout out the answer.

Sister would not look pleased. Her lips would tighten and whiten around the edges when she'd reply, "That is correct."

One day after class, Sister called me aside.

"I realize you know the answers, but you must give the other children a chance," she instructed. "If I want to hear from you, I will call your name, and then you may answer."

"Yes, Sister Paula Francis," I said solemnly.

The next day, more questions. And more answers. Just not from me.

I began my trademark touch-the-floor wave. And finally, yet again, I could stand it no longer. I shouted out the answer.

"That is correct," Sister said. "Now, please march yourself to the cloak closet."

No! Not the dreaded cloak closet!

The cloak closet was where misbehaving children were sent during class. Since I was not one to misbehave, I'd only been in there to hang up my cloak. That's what we were told to call our jackets and coats: Cloaks. We were also taught to raise our hands and ask to "be excused to use the lavatory," should we have an urgent need. Protocol was quite formal at St. Louis Catholic School.

And now, I was being banished to the cloak closet.

She put me in the dark closet and shut the door. I remember this as clearly as if it were yesterday.

I was angry. Not only do I not get called upon to answer any questions, now I must stand in here in the dark cloak closet. Ah, the injustice of it all. I was so mad I began to cry.

And all that crying made it necessary to blow my nose.

But, there is no Kleenex in the cloak closet.

I spied Sister's immaculate black cloak and stopped crying immediately. A devious plan overtook me. I gathered the folds of her cloak to my face, and had a good blow. I hung it back up carefully. I felt much, much better.

I don't know if Sister Paula Francis wondered why I was smiling when she finally opened the closet door.

"Well," she said, "I certainly hope you've learned your lesson."

"Yes, Sister," I said, smiling angelically.

Perhaps she learned hers, too.

— April 2007

"We're on the right road!"

Is it June already? Is school out? Is Mom making lists, while Dad consults the maps?

It's time for summer vacation!

I don't have to dig too far back in my aging mind to remember fondly the Vacations of Summers Past.

Maps? Those were Daddy's job. He would carefully plan a route and then write it down. The map and directions would then become Mom's job. That's where things often fell apart. I recall bouncing around in the backseat – the right side was mine, divided by pillows from "the far side," which was my sister's. (Still today, my sister and I treat vacations differently. Her plans can include sleeping near the Lost River in a tent and riding a mule from campsite to campsite. Mine include down comforters and room service.)

Maps puzzled Mom, but she remained quiet and pleasant during her navigation duties. Daddy? Not so much. Mom would have the maps turned every which way, sometimes upside down. She was small, and often the map was wider than her reach. I guess our favorite bit of family map lore is when Mom happily suggested, "Why don't we swing by and visit Harry and Imogene? It's only two inches out of our way!"

Another memorable observation from Mom was this: She would now and then call out "We're on the right road!" This always startled Daddy and caused him to hit the brakes and, once he realized what she'd said, clench his pipe even tighter in his teeth.

Daddy was also in charge of packing the car. To this day, I have never seen anyone so adept at car packing than my father. I like to think I have followed in his footsteps, but without a family of four to load into a small sedan, I will never know.

As I sit here at my desk, I gaze out on the porch, there is Sanibel Sam. Sam is a 10-foot driftwood stick that looks exactly like some sort of benign sea monster. He rode home from Sanibel with us, his head sticking out one window of our bright orange Hornet, and his tail out the other. It was difficult to enjoy the backseat ride with Sam, but heaven forbid anyone should complain. How Sam, or we, survived the 1,000-mile+ ride, I do not know.

Once, Daddy decreed that we would no longer each have a suitcase for vacation. We'd pack everything in a giant old metal trunk our grandparents gave us. It was lined in bright blue fabric.

It rained mightily during our drive to Okracoke Island. When we reached the Pony Island Motel, Daddy carried that huge trunk up the steps, bent under the weight like some pipe-smoking Sherpa. Imagine our dismay to discover, upon unpacking, that the trunk had leaked and every stitch of clothing was splotched with bright blue stains. Thank heavens tie-dye was just coming into fashion.

I hated Okracoke. There were sand fleas, and crabs, and a seasick-inducing ferry ride to reach our destination. Okracoke offered nothing whatsoever exciting for a 16-year-old. The family vacation lore from that trip is this: "Margo lounged in the room and ate Lifesavers for two weeks." I was indeed addicted to wintergreen Lifesavers at the time. I haven't had one in years, but don't get me started.

We had some excitement about an hour after we checked in. Mom was putting groceries away, and discovered a couple of handguns and some cash stashed in the cupboard. Daddy, Mr. Career Lawman, was beside himself with fervor.

A few hours later, two scruffy dudes knocked on the door. Daddy, wearing his shoulder holster and gold badge (these items traveled everywhere with us), opened it.

"Forget something, fellas?"

"Uh, no … wrong room. Sorry."

No one in our little family will ever forget "The Okracoke Hat." It was a horrid thing, the type of fashion that fathers adore, but that makes teenagers cringe and hide in the room, eating Lifesavers. We detested that hat. Daddy wore it on every subsequent vacation. And, on every subsequent vacation, my sister or I would sneak it into the freezer while he was sleeping.

Thus began a family vacation tradition of freezing various people's possessions overnight. Or worse. One morning, my sister and I awoke to discover our bathing suits were floating in a cooler filled with ice cubes.

For some reason, right this minute, I am sitting here at my computer and I cannot stop laughing.

— June 2010

Daddy Grabs a Bomb

It would have been different in this day and age.

Last night, I heard a story that made me proud.

The heroes were my father, David McCollum, and his best pal, Cliff Nelson.

It was told to me by a woman who observed it all, while shaking in her proverbial boots.

It happened at The Homestead, about 25 years ago.

The hotel was hosting, as it did once or twice a year, for decades, the Business Council.

Sounds innocuous enough, eh?

But actually, the Business Council was a low-key name for a high-stakes summit of this nation's top executives and politicians, who gathered in the mountains to plot the course of America's future. And play golf. The President of the United States was usually on hand. If not he, then the Secretary of State. Richard Nixon, Lyndon Johnson, Henry Kissinger, George Shultz, John Mitchell – all were here at some time with the Business Council.

They gathered twice a year, in May and October – two months where Hot Springs features the best nature has to offer.

So, one stormy May evening about 1982, The Homestead buzzed with the Business Council. The woman, Mary Ellen, was on duty near the front desk in the vast hotel lobby.

Suddenly, she spotted something oddly out of place.

It was a very large, very old, battered black briefcase. It was tucked behind a telephone table in the lobby, almost as if hidden there.

She approached it cautiously and, the more she thought about it, the more suspicious it became.

At that time, the word "terrorism" had only begun to stalk across the minds of most Americans.

But the first thing Mary Ellen thought was, That might be a bomb!

She called Cliff Nelson, the resident manager, and he called Daddy, the chief of security. They were kindly gents, but made quite the fearsome pair when duty called.

They examined the suspect case, and conferred quietly. That was the order of the day back then; hotel guests were at no time to be disturbed, worried or, certainly, thrust into a panic.

Then, Mary Ellen watched as Cliff and Dave picked up the suspicious case and headed out the door. Carrying it gingerly between them, they walked away from the hotel and up the hill. They put it into the trunk of Daddy's car and gently closed the lid.

As Mary Ellen watched, she thought, "There go two of the bravest men I've ever seen."

Knowing my father, he immediately "got on the horn" to Roanoke or Richmond, reporting the suspected bomb. And he certainly conferred with the Secret Service, who were on the premises protecting dignitaries.

But soon, amid the furtive bustle, everything became clear.

The president of General Motors was worried. He was fraught; he was beside himself. Someone, he reported to my father, had stolen his briefcase! It was a treasured possession – a big, old-fashioned black beast he had carried with him since college.

Cliff and Daddy looked at each other, and I'm certain they burst into laughter. I'll bet even the staid Secret Service fellows joined in with relief. The president of GM was giddy with joy, handing out $50 bills as a reward to everyone who had laid eyes or hands on his old briefcase.

In this day and age, no one would have gone near the suspected bomb. The hotel would have been evacuated; far-off squads of armored professionals would have been called, along with dogs and robots. We could have watched the whole thing unfold on CNN.

But back then, it was just Cliff Nelson and Dave McCollum, pipe firmly clenched in his teeth, walking up the hill, hoping they weren't blown to Kingdom Come.

They're both in Kingdom Come now; gone, but not forgotten.

— October 2006

Daddy's Parting Gift

They say that music has the power to soothe the savage beast. I think it's "beast." It could be "the savage breast," but that sounds more like a bad horror movie.

I love to sing. I don't just sing, I belt out tunes. I can do a great Kate Smith, a marvelous Ethel Merman. I didn't have much of a singing voice until, oddly, the day of my father's funeral. Then, it magically arose from somewhere within me, and thank heavens it's still with me today. I think of it as Daddy's Parting Gift.

I sing almost all the time; it surprises people, it perhaps perplexes some, and I'm certain it annoys a few. Some folks crack their knuckles; I sing.

One glorious summer day not long ago, I found myself belting out "Summertime" as I waded in the middle of the Jackson River. There were just two of us – my "oldest" girlfriend and me. And the cows in the meadow. And the fish in the river.

A most-curious thing happened: As I stood there in the Jackson singing "Summertime," fish started jumpin', just like in the song. They leapt everywhere around me. It was startling at first, then a joyful thing that had us laughing and clapping our hands. Some of the fish would actually leap from the water, twist their little heads and look at me, then splash back into the river. Before long, they were swarming around my legs and feet. It was truly a bit of amazing grace, a song they also enjoyed. The herd of cows became quite interested, too, and gathered by the bank, chewing and gaping at us.

My friend and I thought about our fathers, hers a professional fisherman, mine a hobbyist who snagged just one bluegill in his life, and then threw it back. Each of our fathers took us fishing only once in our childhoods. We were, both fathers promptly decreed, entirely too noisy for fishing.

"Pipe down! You're scaring the fish," they each proclaimed.

Well, after what we observed that July day on the Jackson, we beg to differ.

If we had a net or a creel or whatever it is, I bet I could have lured those trout into it with a song. And then thrown them back, so we could do it again.

Here's my on-the-spot adaptation the fish most appreciated:

"Summertime, and the livin' is easy.
Fish are jumpin', and the thistles are high.
The calves are runnin', and their mammas look nervous;
So jump little fishes, leap for the sky.
One of these mornings, you're gonna fly up flashin'
Gonna spread your silver fins, and aim for the sky.
Until that mornin', ain't nothin' gonna harm you.
Relax little fishies, you ain't gonna fry."

    While the fish were content to leap and flash and swim about, the cows had a different reaction. They edged closer and closer to the bank, until some of them decided to wade in and join the party.

    We were not prepared for this: Beasts that must weigh a ton, flies buzzing around their dung-caked faces, plodding deliberately toward us with something resembling a demented smile. Some were "crooning" along with the music.

    The music, believe me, stopped abruptly. We had nowhere to run but downriver, so we hopped in our black rubber tubes and skedaddled.

    The cows followed! We shrieked and splashed and paddled until – Oh, no! – my tube got caught on a river rock and would float no further.

    We were saved by Rose the Bulldog. She'd been snoozing on the bank when the bevy of bovines advanced. She blinked, shook her massive wrinkled head, and then remembered her duty as a bulldog. She barked and darted about, deftly herding our slobbering fans back to the meadow, and then into an even greener pasture. The river reverberated with the thrum of their thundering hooves.

    We relaxed again and, before I even realized what I was doing, I started singing "Wade in the Water." Sure enough, the fish returned, hurling themselves out, casting a swift glance, then splashing down. We decided that, if I were of a mind to, I could hire myself out as a fishing guide.

    Then my friend and I came to a great realization: Our fathers must not have liked to take us noisy girls fishing for one simple reason – we'd spoil the "sport" of it. The livin' would be just a little too easy.

"Just a little fire ..."

It's almost Grampa's birthday.

April Fool!

My late grandfather, David McCollum Sr., had the fortune to be born on April 1. I believe it gave him that certain ability to make people laugh, even long after his death.

The biggest laughs I remember came when Grampa moved to Hot Springs after Gramma died. He came down from Connecticut in an old Nash Rambler station wagon, bag and baggage, and took up residence in the spare bedroom downstairs. I was in high school. Very soon, Grampa's antics became fodder for the little comedy routines I'd perform at school each day.

It reached the point where, as soon as I got off the bus, my friends would gather around and ask, "What did Grampa do yesterday?" The answer always brought fits of teenage laughter.

Consider, for instance, the Case of the Dying Goldfish. For a while there, every day when I came home from school, at least one of my goldfish would be floating dead on the top of the tank. It was a curious mystery. Until, that is, the fateful day I came home from school sick. Grampa was taking his nap, and did not know I'd returned early. In midafternoon, I came downstairs to get some juice. As I rounded the landing, I had a clear view of the breakfast nook where the fish tank stood.

There was Grampa. He had my flute in his hand, and was using it to stir up the fish tank. Round and round he stirred, in a rather furious motion. The bright blue gravel swirled about, and the fish darted madly, crashing into the side of the glass.

"Grampa!" I cried. "Stop! You'll kill the fish!"

He looked surprised to see me, but kept stirring.

"Oh, no," he said. "They like it; gives 'em some excitement."

Grampa didn't have much to do, so he became an avid TV fan. It did not matter what was on, Grampa would sit in his chair, fervently smoking Camels, and watch. My father, no big TV fan, would roll his eyes and exclaim, "Cripes, Dad – you're watching a cooking show!"

My father had little patience at times and, despite being a famed jokester himself, did not happily suffer the shenanigans of others. Daddy was the only one who was not amused that night, at the Sunday dinner table, when Grampa dragged his sleeve through the mustard, and then went into contortions trying to lick it off.

One afternoon while Mom was fixing lunch, Grampa shuffled out to the kitchen. His manner of walking was to take very short, very quick steps; all of us except Mom would mimic him when he wasn't looking, and then we'd laugh.

So, Grampa shuffled out, got a small saucepan, and filled it with water. Mom figured he was making himself some tea, but then Grampa shuffled out of the kitchen, carrying the small pan of water. Mom and I looked at each other quizzically. Soon, he shuffled back with the empty pan, filled it, and again crept toward the living room.

On his next trip back with the empty pan, Mom inquired, "Grampa, can I help you?"

"Oh, it's nothing Dotty," he said. "Just a little fire in here, just a little fire."

Fortunately, my father was home and was able to pick up the flaming easy chair and throw it out the front door onto the lawn. Again, he was not amused.

Grampa is long gone, but never forgotten.

Sunday night, my mother, sister and I were having dinner. My sister got up to get something. She shuffled toward the kitchen, taking very short, very quick steps.

"It's nothing," she said. "Just a little fire in here, just a little fire."

— April 2001

Flying Miss Daisy

I just returned from Paradise.
Paradise, Vermont.
Imagine my surprise when I arrived at my old pal's new house, and discovered she really did live in Paradise. There was a sign to prove it. Flying to Paradise, however, was none too heavenly. I spend a lot of time as a companion to dogs. Dogs are ideal companions, and I like to think I return that favor.

The Vermont trip was my first venture into human companionship, so to speak. In return for my all-expense paid jaunt, I accompanied a dear elderly lady who is unable to travel alone. I had misgivings. I'm not a "people person." I'm essentially one of those "loners" you read about, albeit one with no bodies buried in the basement. Thus I embarked on an adventure I like to call "Flying Miss Daisy."

Miss Daisy is an elegant, cultured, lovely woman whose mind likes to take a vacation just as much as she does.

We were driven to the Roanoke airport in a Lincoln Town Car, which Miss Daisy owns but never drives. I had concerns about the stringent new security measures. Still, I figured that two nicely dressed older women with lots of matching luggage did not fit a terrorist profile.

Apparently, I was wrong.

The ticket agent accepted our bags without a single question about who packed them, or what they contained. "This is a breeze!" I thought.

We waited in the airport restaurant until 30 minutes before our departure time. The Roanoke airport is small and friendly, I thought; there's no reason to rush down to the less-comfortable chairs at the gate, when we can sit here and sip cappuccino.

Wrong, again.

The next ticket agent was less accommodating. He demanded our identification. As I showed my driver's license, it hit me: Miss Daisy hasn't driven for years; did she even have a license? We scrabbled through every scrap of paper in her designer handbag. There were cards for doctors and the Greenbrier Golf and Tennis Club and her hairdresser. There were about 50 family photographs, most yellowed with age.

"A photo ID," repeated the unbending clerk.

"Here I am!" Miss Daisy said triumphantly, showing him a picture taken in Switzerland in 1964.

The clerk was not satisfied.

On our second pass through the scraps of her life, we found an old driver's license. He accepted it, and we were on to step two: Screening.

I sailed through the machines. Miss Daisy did not.

Stern-faced government agents hauled her off to the side. I was not allowed to join her.

"She's confused," I pleaded.

"This will only take a moment, ma'am. Wait here."

A female agent took off Miss Daisy's coat. And her belt. And her shoes. And then, her sweater. The dear, doe-eyed Miss Daisy stood there in her undershirt and chic slacks, as the agent repeatedly passed a wand over her body.

Meanwhile, male agents rifled through her train case, inspecting an array of medicines and red lipstick. They stopped at her toenail clippers, and had a conference about whether she would be allowed to retain this potential implement of terror.

"What's happening?" Miss Daisy inquired.

"They're afraid you might give the pilot a pedicure," I replied wryly.

Agents were not amused.

Finally, we were allowed to trot toward the gate. As we did so, we heard our names announced over the loudspeaker. The plane was about to depart. We ran. Thankfully, Miss Daisy is still quite spry.

The departure area was empty. The plane sat on the tarmac, its propellers spinning.

"We made it!" we shouted.

Not yet.

Again, I sailed through.

Again, Miss Daisy was intercepted.

Again, she was hauled off, half-stripped down, and wanded by agents.

Changing planes in Pittsburgh, an airport teeming with thousands of travelers, Miss Daisy again drew suspicion that warranted intense inspection.

I was as confused as she.

Apparently, elegant elderly Caucasian ladies fit some sort of subversive profile. I ask you, when was the last time a woman – of any age or social standing – hijacked an airplane? A pastry cart, perhaps, but never an airplane.

— December 2002

Babies, Boomer and Rutabaga, Too!

If you've never visited the Highland County Fair, you should do yourself a favor and plan a trip to "Virginia's Little Switzerland" the last weekend in August.

It is so pure, so true, so filled with the potential for nostalgia.

It's life as many of us once knew it, and life as we all should know it at least once.

Farm wives compete for ribbons with floral arrangements, hand-sewn aprons, homemade jams and fluffy biscuits. Gardeners exhibit gargantuan homegrown gourds. The lambs and the piglets are in pens built to accommodate petting, although that must be done surreptitiously. Yet, as you stare into the soulful eyes of a fuzzy Dorset, try not to think where it will be next week.

The biggest crowd pleasers seem to be the Demolition Derby on Thursday night, and the Friday night Tractor Pull. I've never attended either event. I can experience the vicarious thrill of the Demolition Derby just by trying to exit the Dollar General parking lot. And I don't want to meet the guy who's big and burly enough to pull a tractor around.

I know a foursome of fellows from Washington, D.C. who come down for the Highland County fair every year, just to get their "fix" of rural America at its best. Georgetown may offer tasty tapas and tuna carpaccio, but the fair provides its own epicurean delights: Cotton candy, corn dogs, and maple-flavored barbecue.

Back when I was a reporter for the newspaper that serves Highland and Bath counties, I had a fair assignment every summer. Every year, I'd grumble to myself all the way to Monterey, and smile to myself all the way home.

The first year, I covered the sheep costume contest.

Now, if ever an event begged for feature coverage, this is it.

The pressing question, of course, is this: Who dressed like whom?

Well, the farm kids who raised the sheep dressed them up like people.

I fondly recall "Lambo" – decked out in camouflage overalls and green beret, two ammo belts slung across his flanks.

There was a "Geisheepa" in a kimono and obi sash, an ovine "Clown Prince," even a Professor Charles Lamb, in a jacket with elbow patches, smoking a pipe.

Another year I, the only childless member of the local press, was assigned to cover the "Cutest Baby Contest."

Why anyone would agree to the no-win prospect of judging one baby cuter than another is a question I can't answer.

The baby contest was a sight for eyes and ears I won't soon forget.

They cooed, they gooed, they boo-hoo-hooed. They crawled, they squalled, they dribbled and drooled. Babies of every description and demeanor were trekked across the stage by their proud mothers.

I especially recall the mother who had the, well, let's call it courage, to display her four-day-old infant. She dangled the teensy baby, which seemed to weigh about 12 ounces, in front of the crowd. Its skin was purple. Its miniscule mouth gaped in a toothless, silent scream. I didn't blame it one bit for being angry.

One time at the fair, I had the unsettling honor of standing in a stall with a 2,000-pound Black Angus bull named Boomer. He was better groomed than I and, thank heavens, weighed more. At one point, his highly-polished hoof strayed atop my white clog, in which rested my foot. Why I wore white clogs to a livestock show, I cannot tell you. Why I'm still walking today is a mystery, too.

At one point, Boomer turned his massive, curly head toward me. I drew back, but since he took up most of the stall, there was nowhere to cower from the bull. Boomer rested his head on my shoulder. He sighed. He looked up at me with the biggest brown eyes I've ever seen, and fluttered the world's longest black lashes.

I could not eat a cheeseburger for months.

— September 2002

Of Pasta and Panic

One thing most of us in rural locales don't much bother with is fancy alarm systems.

For some, a slavering hound dog under the porch has proven an effective burglar alarm. Others might prefer to let the burglar enter the house. Then, instead of the annoying beep of an activated alarm, the interloper hears the unmistakable sound of a shotgun being cocked. This, too, is an effective deterrent to mischief and mayhem.

Out here in the country, "casing the joint" doesn't work, either. We all know who drives what, when, and why. There's no such thing as unnoticed comings and goings; usually, we know where you're headed, or where you've been: "There they are, home from church." "There she goes, off to the beauty parlor." Prospective burglars who think they can cruise slowly up and down the road without attracting attention should know this: Someone's already called the sheriff. And loaded the shotgun.

I get real nervous when I visit city folks with alarm systems. This stems from one very unfortunate incident at my cousin's fabulous spread in Old Saybrook, Connecticut. It's one of the wealthiest communities in the country; those who live there don't mess around with rinky-dink alarm systems, or cranky coon dogs.

My cousin and her husband had gone to a party that evening, leaving me, my mother, and my frail, aged Aunt Elsie alone in the sprawling mansion. We'd prepare a nice dinner, and laugh about happy memories. The table was set, the pasta steaming, the wine poured. I decided to dim the dining room lights. There were lots of switches and such on the wall; I tried several, but couldn't find the dimmer. I noticed an odd switch with a little red button in the center. This must be it, I thought.

Even as my finger pressed it, my brain screamed "NO!"

What did I know from a panic button? A cacophonous, frightening siren filled the house and echoed into the yard. A disembodied voice commanded, "Leave the area immediately! The police have been called."

I ran outside, wringing my hands, seeking assistance from kindly neighbors. Instead, well-dressed matrons and captains of industry eyed me suspiciously. They were all apparently departing for the same black-tie affair, their luxury sedans purring in front of groomed estates.

I adopted my "confused country girl" persona. "Help me!" I cried. "We're from the hills of Virginia! We were just trying to dim the lights!"

Two dapper gentlemen in tuxedos strolled up the driveway. One held a martini in his manicured hand. With a sardonic smile, he inquired, "Is there a problem here?"

The siren continued to scream. The forceful, gruff voice continued to command that we leave the area immediately.

"I only wanted to dim the lights," I babbled. "I hit this little button. Please help me turn it off!"

The gentlemen looked at one another knowingly. "The panic button," they nodded in unison.

"The what?" I wondered.

I could hear police sirens in the distance. We entered the house, and the gentlemen looked at the flashing display of electronic doodads.

"What's the code?" they inquired.

"The what?"

Soon, there were five of us in the tiny space. Aunt Elsie, leaning on her cane, stood rooted in front of the blinking panels. Her glasses were askew. Her mouth moved, but no words came forth. Finally, she uttered, "I can't breathe."

Two policemen burst into the fray, hands on their holsters. I spit out my story as succinctly as I could. They didn't buy it.

"What's the code?" they demanded.

"The what?"

The officers explained that, in order to quell the infernal siren, we had to punch in a numeric code.

We called my cousin's daughter in Arizona. She divulged the secret code. The police punched it on the pad. Blessed silence ensued.

The excitement was not over, however. Aunt Elsie, who had so looked forward to spending the weekend away from the nursing home, was in a pale, sweating dither. "My heart is racing," she panted. "Put me in bed."

It was my duty to explain the evening's debacle when my cousin returned home. She checked on Aunt Elsie immediately. The exciting experience had dampened the poor dear's zeal for life in the real world. She pleaded to be returned to the nursing home first thing the next morning. She noted there was no need for me to go along for the ride.

— *May 2003*

An Alarming Trip to the Big City

I went to Richmond over Labor Day to visit some friends, eat Greek and Mexican food, and visit the Virginia Museum of Fine Arts. We traipsed cobblestone streets, and browsed the boutiques of Cary Town.

It was a weekend filled with things I love to do whenever I'm in a Big City. I had always thought of myself as a city girl; but, when I moved back to Bath County from San Francisco, I started to realize the truth: I prefer the rural country life.

I was reminded of that again during my jaunt to Richmond. Despite its museums, restaurants, clubs and shopping opportunities, there are things about city living that just don't jibe with me anymore.

And the greatest of those is this: The near-manic quest for security. Sure, hurtling down an eight-lane interstate, looking for exits and merging correctly without incident, is a gripping experience I can live without; but, that security thing really pushes my panic button.

I panicked again Labor Day weekend. My hosts and I had retired for the evening, in our respective rooms of a fabulous, sprawling house, landscaped with goldfish ponds, rare lilies and towering poplar trees. I couldn't sleep, and figured I'd step outside on the patio, get some fresh air, and listen to the sounds of the night. It would, I hoped, relax me.

I unlocked the door and tried to pull it open. It seemed stuck. I tried again, more forcefully. Open it came, accompanied with a deafening, pulsating alarm that pierced the night. I slammed the door, hoping the cacophony would subside. It did not.

I ran upstairs, wringing my hands and screaming, "I'm sorry! I was just stepping outside! What's happening? Make it stop!"

Big lights around the outside perimeter of the house were flashing. My host stumbled from his bedroom, rubbing his eyes. He tripped over a decorative tropical plant in the hallway. He was no longer the happy host I'd known for decades.

Limping, at as brisk a pace as he could muster, he headed for a command control center in the kitchen that had puzzled me since my arrival. He punched in six or seven numbers, using his other hand as a shield so that, I guess, I would not become privy to the secret sequence of codes. I guess city folks don't trust anyone.

Blessed silence ensued. And then the phone rang.

"That will be the police," he said grimly.

"The police? Tell me the police aren't coming!" I cried.

He answered the call and, oddly, spoke not in words, but in numbers.

"Seven, two, four," I heard him say as a form of greeting. Then a pause, followed by six-one-zero-three-nine."

(In case you're planning to go to Richmond and invade my friend's home, be advised that I've made up these numbers.)

I should have known that the perplexing pad of lights and numbers were the key to some sort of security system. I'd seen my host dashing for that pad every time we entered the house. In my country-girl ignorance, I figured it was some sort of citified answering machine. I should have known a house like that, in a city like that, would be wired for potential Armageddon. I should have known, because every car of every city friend I know is also wired. From a half-block away, they pull out a little doodad, punch a button and, voila, the car magically unlocks itself. The same holds true for locking the car – we walk away, they pull out the little doodad and punch the button. The car emits an eerie sound, as if a large man had stepped on a small puppy, and the doors lock themselves.

This is all very curious to a country girl who leaves her keys in the ignition, so she doesn't have to waste time looking for them. My home security system consists of a suspicious cat who, whenever a car pulls into the driveway, darts to the windowsill and growls. The last time the police showed up at my house, they were returning a wallet I'd left at the fried Oreo concession at the Millboro carnival.

— September 2000

Ask Auntie Margo

Welcome to "Ask Auntie Margo," an advice column for those who love their pets. While Auntie Margo will attempt to answer every question, she will by no means be responsible for the validity of her answers.

Q: Dear Auntie Margo: Will you keep our dogs while we're on vacation? We're concerned they will miss us terribly.

A: Wise up! Your dogs will love me as much as they do you, as soon as I waltz in and give them biscuits.

Q: Dear Auntie Margo: Will you keep my cat while I'm away? She is very cuddly and loveable. I want to make sure she isn't lonely while I'm gone. Her name is (insert one: Stinker Butt. Crappy Kitty. Mole Breath.)

A: I don't know why people insist on giving cats such awful names. The first thing I will do is give your cat a respectable, even cute, name. The cat won't appreciate it, but I will feel much better.

The short answer is, yes, I will keep your cat. The truth is, the cat will not care. Your cat may be cuddly and loveable while you're at home, but as soon as Auntie Margo arrives, it will turn recalcitrant and snarly. During the 30 seconds per day when I actually see your elusive darling, it will hiss, claw, and bite. I must often seek medical care while I am keeping cats. Cats have injured me more often than rattlesnakes.

Q: Dear Auntie Margo: Are you afraid of anything?

A: Rattlesnakes! I believe Auntie Margo exudes some special pheromone that snakes find attractive, even irresistible. Two years ago, dogs and I were attacked when we disturbed two mating rattlesnakes. I did not feel their pain and humiliation. I was just plain scared stiff. I looked down at my feet and willed them to run, yet I could not move. Last year, a snarly, recalcitrant cat I was keeping found a snake in the house! I could not move. The house was modern, well-built, and sealed for central air-conditioning. Still, the interloper sensed that special pheromone, and slithered inside with mayhem in mind.

Last week, two dogs and I passed by a compost pile in which a five-foot rattlesnake was lurking. We were happy because we were ignorant. Ten minutes later, another dog found the snake; his mistress (the dog's, not the snake's) was scared stiff. She called a sharp-shooting neighbor who blew off the snake's head. Thirty minutes later, it was still writhing, shaking the 12 rattles on its tail.

Q: Dear Auntie Margo: Will you be walking in the woods anytime soon?

A: Not until I've got to wear snow boots.

Q: Dear Auntie Margo: Are ticks a big concern?

A: They were, until I encountered the snakes.

Q: Dear Auntie Margo: Our pets do not like "people food." Can we count on you to uphold our "pet-food only" policy?

A: Probably not. Your pets have proven to have sneaky habits, such as snarfing an entire tray of fresh-baked cookies as soon as my back is turned. Your dog slurped down a steaming cup of cappuccino while I was making your bed. Your cat stole and devoured a piece of fried chicken while I was answering your phone.

Q: Dear Auntie Margo: Is there anything a pet will not eat?

A: Not to my knowledge. A cat I know enjoys eating beets. A dog I know likes spinach soufflé, although the aftereffects are rather unpleasant.

Q: Dear Auntie Margo: Will you care for my turtle while I'm away? He's no trouble at all.

A: I would really rather not. I am still smarting from that time last summer when I somehow murdered Bob the Goldfish. I love dogs, and I will tolerate your cat, but please refrain from subjecting unusual pets to Auntie Margo's care. I am currently "caring for" a turtle named Cleo. It's difficult to tell, but I think she may be dead.

Q: Dear Auntie Margo: What would you do if my dog sneaked a half-dead groundhog into the house?

A: First, I would rebuff the dog's efforts to lick me in a demonstration of joy and victory. Then, I would begin searching for a snow shovel. Finally, I would seriously consider filling the food and water dishes, and packing my bags.

Q: Dear Auntie Margo: Is there any special little thank-you gift we could bring you from (insert one: Scotland, Bermuda, Kansas City)?

A: How about a lovely snakeskin purse?

— August 2004

Revenge of the Critters

You can prove it by me: This spring has brought The Revenge of The Creatures.

It's not a new Pixar movie. Rather, it's a perplexing phenomenon of nature.

I had a very busy day ahead last Friday. That's why it was especially disconcerting to be awakened at 4:44 a.m. – way too early, even for me – by the clang and clatter of metal hitting concrete.

Since I was now "awake," I decided to march into the kitchen and holler at a bunch of raccoons out by the garbage can. Brownie and I hustled through the darkened house. Brownie was the lucky one; a dog cannot stub its toe. And, to my knowledge, a dog has never subsequently tripped over a human.

Hopping and cursing, I banged loudly on the kitchen door. The garbage can sits just outside. I was afraid that, if I actually opened the door to holler, the raccoons would somehow muscle their way inside. That simply would not do.

We marched back to bed and snuggled down to sleep. Ten minutes later, the danged clanging began anew, accompanied by dragging sounds.

I stomped out there again and banged, but then, by the faintest light of dawn, I could see trash strewn across the backyard.

Fully awake now, I turned on the lights, found some rubber gloves and slippers, and made my way outside. I am glad that no neighbors can see me up on the hill. Surely, an angry woman in pajamas and rubber gloves, muttering and storming around the backyard at 5 in the morning, might be cause for alarm.

I have figured out a way to perhaps deter the raccoons. I can't imagine what it is in my garbage that's attracting them, but now, I make a point of removing my nail polish each week, just after I've emptied the garbage, and putting the stinky little cotton balls full of acetone into the can. So far this week, so good.

Yesterday, I heard that a black bear has been marauding through downtown Hot Springs in broad daylight. He has apparently checked out the hotel swimming pool, surely scaring guests from the suburbs. He has torn down and made off with entire feeders full of birdseed. He has trampled through the flower beds of garden club ladies.

I think he made a "deposit" in my driveway. I am not certain, because

I've nothing to compare it to, but let's just say it is quite a hefty and unusual-looking deposit that intrigues both Brownie and me. I've known some huge dogs in my day, but never one who could create something like this.

And now for today's revenge. This morning, I am blithely carrying my coffee from the kitchen to the office when something quite odd catches my eye. It seems to be a leaf. It seems to be stuck to my living room window.

Upon further inspection, I discover it is a bat. A bat who has managed to squeeze itself between the screen and the storm window. In my living room.

I tapped on the window to awaken him, in hopes he was some slugabed adolescent who'd fly back to his real home. But no. It is now afternoon, and he appears to be in no hurry whatsoever to leave. Yippee.

— June 2009

The Critters Have Their Say

I'm exhausted. I'll let the others have their say.

BROWNIE: I am very tired. I get no sleep. I am way too busy trembling and hiding underneath the bed. There are far too many brilliant flashes of light, followed by deep, very scary booms. I spend all night jumping onto the bed, panting loudly, whining, and then jumping down, only to repeat the process.

On the bright side, there are wondrous things happening from sunup until sundown. Every morning at the crack of dawn, we are awakened by clanging. We hop up and go outside in our pajamas. One of us wears rubber gloves. Outside is a wonderland of aromatic garbage. Wednesday's steak fat, along with uneaten potatoes, and that ham she threw out just because it had a rainbow glaze. She curses the raccoons. I can hear them giggling.

When we walk down the driveway, there it is: The big pile of very black "doo." I find it endlessly intriguing. I can't wait to meet whoever did it. My tail wags at the thought.

BOB the BAT: Cripes! A fella can't get a decent day's sleep around here. I'm a loner. Now that I've found a perfect place – squeezed flat between the screen and the storm window – I am constantly interrupted by tapping on the window. Then, she goes outside and peers at me from there. I heard her say she thinks I'm kinda cute. Then she worries I'll get inside and make a nest in her hair. All I want is some shut eye! Is that too much to ask?

THURSTON the RACCOON: Howdy there. I'm the Granddaddy of this bunch, and I gotta tell ya, we are commandos! Every morning about four o'clock, we scamper onto the back porch. We work as a team – me, my sons, their wives, and all the little nippers. I weigh the most, so I clamber up top and start rocking. The younger ones surround the can and do the shaking, while the nippers gather on one side and push. Hard. Success every time!

While it's not necessary, it's fun to shred the black plastic bag. Then, we rummage through the contents. And always, we are disappointed. Strawberry hulls? Bad ham? Flaccid french fries? Cuban coffee grounds? Caramba! Who needs it?

Sometimes, she stomps through the house and pounds on the back door. As if that would deter us! We spread as much as we can, as far as we can. Then, we go into the woods and wait. When the sun rises, she'll come out in mismatched pajamas, her hair wildly awry, wearing rubber shoes and gloves. We can hear her muttering. She can't hear us giggling, though. Tee hee.

BRUNO the BEAR: It's getting more and more difficult to make it. Times are tough. Condos and houses are going up throughout the woods; a self-respecting bear has very little privacy. Besides, I just woke up from a long winter's nap, and I'm hawngry. I prowl, but what do I find? A stagnant pond filled with clear blue water, surrounded by THEM. In silly little suits, floating on foamy "fun noodles." The only fun is, they all scream and grab their children and dash away when I lumber onto the scene.

Bird seed. That's all I want. And maybe a honeycomb, and few flowers and herbs. I'm reduced to scrounging through backyards. Believe me, a feeder full of expensive seed is barely a snack for me.

But then, there's HER yard. Not a spec of birdseed in sight. A seemingly nice picnic, though, until you notice the ham is moldy and the fries are flaccid.

I'll show her. Ah, right here in the driveway where she walks that silly dog ought to be a good place. Ahhhhhhh. Take that, you non-feeder of birds! Heh, heh, heh.

— June 2009

The Dreaded Drone of Danger

This spring, I whined and moaned about ladybugs.
Ha! What did I know?
I'd give anything to have the ladybugs back, if only they'd replace the hornets.

I have learned a few lessons about hornets this summer. It's a very swift learning process.

For instance, I've learned that hornets can make nests in the ground. I've learned never to walk around outside barefoot. Ever.

I've learned that there is truly nothing that can alleviate a hornet's sting. The searing, all-encompassing, relentless pain is there for most of the day.

Last week, when ground-dwelling hornets stung my finger as I walked past, my mind raced as I sped into the house.

Is it ammonia that you pour on the sting? Is it baking soda? Is it vinegar? Is it lye?

I tried everything but the lye, and still nothing made the horrid ache abate.

I've learned that hornets can get angry for no reason.
I've learned that, once enraged, they will follow you.
I've learned that, unlike wasps, hornets don't stop stinging.
While watering the shrubs this week, I learned the true meaning of the phrase "mad as a wet hornet."

I hate hornets.

And now, I'm plagued with them. It almost makes me long for the locusts.

As soon as the early summer sun began to shine, I began to notice large, angry hornets in my house. They're hard to ignore, actually. First, there's the insistent, low-decibel drone. Hornets have apparently mastered the perpetual-motion thing.

While one may sleep through the morning alarm, a hornet's drone is the death knell for dreamland.

I'm ashamed to admit I cower from hornets. I wish they would just go away, but they do not. They careen crazily about the room. It's impossible to focus on anything but the buzz of imminent danger.

How, I wondered, are they getting in here? Why won't they just stay outside?

But no. Five or six big hornets per day drone drunkenly around my living room.

I finally faced my fears and went on the offense. Now, I'm a killing machine. Armed with a can of hornet spray and a stiff-heeled slipper, I hunt them down. They're easy to find. They're attracted to the windows. If they're so anxious to get out, why did they come inside?

I sneak up on the buzzing offenders and drench them in poison. They do a death dance. I should feel bad. But I don't. I cover their nasty little black and yellow faces with toxic foam. I happily watch them writhe and, finally, die.

I've learned it is important to let a "dead" hornet lie there for a day before picking it up to put in the trash. It seems the stinger is the last thing to go.

Friends advised me to stroll around the house and look for the hornet's nest. Now, that's something I didn't really relish. But, high in the eaves, there it was. It seemed too small for all the hornets I'd seen. Then, I combed the insecticide aisle in the supermarket, looking for something absolutely lethal. One label promised to kill hornets from up to 22 feet away. I'd have preferred 40, even 30, feet of distance, but 22 would have to do.

To kill hornets, one must wait until the still of the night.

I longed for night-vision goggles. I longed for that service I'd call "Rent a Husband." After all, someone should be standing inside, peering out, phone at the ready to call 9-1-1.

But it was only I, shaking but determined, clad in an attractive nightgown (just in case the rescue squad was summoned), armed with a can of deadly foam. The cats watched the spectacle intently. But neither of them can operate the phone.

The mission was successful, and surprisingly easy. I want to do it again. And again.

I'm reminded of my favorite commercial; I think it's for an insurance company: Two guys are taking down a big hornet's nest. Doofus #1 teeters on a tree limb, armed with a broomstick to knock the nest into a garbage can held by the other. The plan is for the nest to drop into the can, whereupon Doofus #2 quickly claps on the lid. Naturally, hilarious mayhem ensues.

At least, I used to think it was hilarious. Now, the idea makes a little more sense to me.

— July 2005

No Bother At All

During a recent housesitting stint, I did my best to care for a blind, deaf, aged English sheepdog named Candy. In her prime, Candy was a show-stopper. Today, she bears close watching.

It was, I imagine, a lot like working in a nursing home. One must assure the clients are amply fed and watered, administer medications, and sigh with relief during their frequent bouts of napping. I was forewarned that Candy was "a little gassy." I imagine this, too, is a common malady among her 98-year-old human counterparts.

A funny thing about dog-sitting is this: You get the low-down in small doses. In this case, I knew Candy was blind. A day later I learned of the deafness. An hour before the stint began, the gas problem was mentioned. And, as I'm hauling my stuff in the door, an entirely new situation is revealed: Because Candy's dog door must remain open at all times, a neighborhood raccoon has made the place a frequent stop along its scavenging route. And if, by some chance, the entry is barred, the raccoon peeks through the glass and knocks on the door.

I discovered this gradual-revelation theorem earlier this summer. With more than a little trepidation, I agreed to sit for four – count 'em, four! – little dogs in a nearby town. I like big dogs. I can handle two of them, no problem. Little dogs are another story. Little dogs make big noises, in high, yappy voices. And their owner did acknowledge, during that first conversation, that the dogs were noisy.

Still, I like the dogs' owners, and figured I was certainly capable of herding and corralling their small, noisy brood.

I always make an initial foray to the sitting site before the owners leave town. I need to know the whereabouts of food, water and treats; I need to let the dogs sniff me; I need to learn how to operate the satellite TV.

Shortly before my visit, the owner stopped by and happened to mention "the construction." Now, one of my chief bugaboos about housesitting is construction. I do this to pretend I'm on a vacation with pets, not to endure teams of workmen traipsing about at an early hour.

"That must be a hassle," I said, hoping to sound sympathetic rather than selfish.

"Yeah," he replied. "We'll just be glad to stop sleeping in the living room."

"Uh, I'll be sleeping in the living room?"

"Yes, but don't worry; the dogs will keep you company."

"Uh, the dogs sleep in the bed?"

"They're no bother."

"Anything else I should know?"

He mentioned the two cats. And "old, blind Buddy."

"Old Blind Buddy?"

"Yeah, he's 17. He lives outside, though. He's no bother."

OK. We've got four spoiled little dogs, two cats, and old blind Buddy.

I arrived for my initial visit already wishing I could back out of the obligation.

Then I discovered Thumper, the bunny who lives in the dining room. And two fish.

"I know nothing about bunnies or fish."

"Oh, they're no bother."

They were leaving town that moment; it was too late to make excuses. I'll stick it out, I promised myself. How difficult could it be?

I was bitten twice upon arrival, as I tried to make my way in the door. The angry little dogs were having none of it; they yapped and screamed and skittered and snarled. The bunny seemed depressed. The cats yowled piteously. Old blind Buddy gripped his empty water bowl tightly in his jaws, staring hopefully through sightless eyes. Only the fish seemed carefree.

Barely able to think through the din, I tried to settle in. Soon, a terrific thunderstorm struck, terrifying the animals and zapping the power. All four dogs leaped into my chair and, within seconds, I felt a warm liquid flowing across my lap.

I made it through just one night. With the owners' approval, I subcontracted the job to a 13-year-old boy who seemed eager for the opportunity.

Maybe I'm not such a professional pet-sitter, after all.

— July 2003

Snooping with Dogs

I spend a lot of time living in other people's houses while they're out of town.

And, while it's never been mentioned to me, I think I know their greatest qualm.

Snooping.

I know that, on the rare occasions when someone else has stayed in my place to feed the cats, I've feared they might snoop through all my drawers.

Not that there's anything salacious or exciting or illegal lurking amongst my underwear, t-shirts or towels. Those things are just, well, private.

I imagine, before I've "moved in" the first time, the couple lies in bed the night before and wonders aloud, "Do you think she'll snoop through our drawers?"

"Better hide the such-and-such," the husband might say.

"And what about the doo-dad?" the wife might giggle.

"Hide everything," the husband will pronounce.

Of course, if I were the type to go snooping through drawers, the such-and-such and the doo-dads would surely be discovered.

But I am definitely not the type.

In fact, my greatest housesitting qualm is that I'll have to open the drawers to look for something.

I am meticulous about not opening drawers.

The kitchen, of course, is fair game. Believe me, if I've sat in your house, I know where every single kitchen item is by the time you reach Charlottesville. I know where you keep the bread knife, the mixer, and the maple syrup.

But that's the extent of it. If I'm sitting at your computer and need a pencil, I'll go get one from my purse, rather than open your desk drawer.

Until, that is, I need something important.

One such situation comes to mind.

In a big house in the middle of nowhere one night, the electricity went out; I needed a flashlight, candles, matches. Now, I not only had to snoop through drawers and closets, I had to do it in the dark.

I managed to find three big flashlights, the kind with those bulky square batteries. None worked. I groped about the pantry, and found a spare battery. Trouble was, it required some knowledge to insert. There was a squiggly, pointed copper thing on one end, and I couldn't, in pitch darkness, figure out how it fit into the scheme of things.

Finally, I crept into the dining room and found some candles. Now, for the matches.

Finding matches in the home of non-smokers takes some doing.

It was not to happen for me that night.

I thought about where I keep a flashlight: My bedroom nightstand.

Opening bedroom nightstand drawers is an absolute no-no in my housesitting etiquette. Still, the situation called for desperate measures.

I skulked into the couple's bedroom. There were two nightstands. I stood there for awhile before I got up the gumption to open one drawer and feel around.

Then I laughed out loud: What, I wondered, if I found what I thought was a flashlight and turned it on, only to feel it begin to buzz?

But there were no long, cylindrical objects in that drawer.

I stumbled over to the other nightstand and repeated the process.

No cylindrical objects there, either.

Finally, I decided my only option was to go to bed, regardless of the fact that it was just 8:30.

The dogs and I spent a cold, dark winter night tossing and shivering and sighing in the bedroom. We awoke before first light, ready to greet another day.

That morning, the couple called.

I gave a full report of the previous night's nerve-wracking activities, leaving out my little joke about the nightstand.

"Where do you keep the flashlight, anyway?" I asked.

"It's just to the left of the sofa, on the hearth," the wife said.

I laughed out loud again.

I'd been sitting on that sofa when the electricity failed. Had I simply reached out my left hand, a working flashlight would have been the first thing I grasped.

— March 2003

Like Cats and Dogs

Well, it's the holiday shopping season.
Each year, it seems, my list dwindles.
But this time around, that has changed.
I now have someone new to lavish extravagant gifts upon: My little dog Brownie.
After years of loving and caring for dogs of others, "Auntie Margo" has a dog of her own.
I'd been looking for my own dog for months. I got tired of waiting for the cats to die, and decided they would have to learn to live with it. One obliged me by immediately passing away; I miss her every day, but my life quickly got a lot easier.
But then there's ZuZu. ZuZu isn't obliging anyone by doing anything. She's a pulchritudinous pussycat who's anything but a pussycat. She is grumpy and recalcitrant and snarly. She had a hissy fit the day Brownie arrived, and has yet to forgive the supreme insult of having to share.
Brownie had been living with a dear lady who had to go into the nursing home. I got an email plea from the kind ladies at the Bath Animal Welfare Foundation. Would someone be interested in picking up a little dog, Brownie, from the shelter and bringing her to the nursing home to visit her lady?
I could do that, I thought.
Since my mother passed away last year, she's been busy, busy, busy in heaven, sending me good deeds to do. I was stubborn at first, but have learned that good deeds bring their own incomparable rewards. Now, I go looking for them.
By the time I volunteered to try, for one day, taking Brownie to the nursing home, she had already left the shelter. Her vet had learned Brownie was there, and hired the personable little dog as a greeter at the animal hospital.
The first day went wonderfully well. The dear old lady was thrilled to see the dog.
"Is that my little Brownie?" she cried. "Come here and sit on Mama's lap!"
Brownie happily obliged.
The lady can't remember her husband's name – "I should know that," she pondered when I asked – but, by golly, she can't forget her dog.

Funny, but every lady I chat with when I'm up there has forgotten her husband's name, but can recall every dog she ever had.

Fellas, what does that tell you?

By the second day we left the nursing home, I looked over at Brownie and told her, "You're coming home with me!"

ZuZu immediately established her supremacy. I bought Brownie a nice little bed, which ZuZu sleeps in, day and night. I bought Brownie some toys. ZuZu, who never cared one whit for playthings, now tosses them around with gay abandon.

Brownie gives ZuZu a wide berth. She hangs her head and skulks past the hissing cat, often taking a circuitous route under the bed, or behind the sofa.

One morning, Brownie, ZuZu and I were in the kitchen together, making coffee. I clumsily stumbled over the cat, stomping on her tail.

ZuZu let loose an ungodly feline scream.

I glanced at Brownie.

Moments before, she had been cowering in the corner.

But, if a dog can laugh, that is surely what Brownie did next.

Her whole body wagged. Her little lips were pulled back in a big, happy smile. I swear, she actually chuckled.

I bent down to apologize to ZuZu. This was a fruitless endeavor.

ZuZu continued to complain, switching her tail in the air.

Right then, Brownie dashed over and pushed her doggie nose into the inviting aperture.

I laughed so hard, I discovered I was wide-awake without the coffee.

That's one of the wonderful things about having a dog: You can wake up and start each day with a hearty laugh.

I've had to make adjustments, though. No longer can I just hop off for a day of shopping and lunch. No longer can I take a few days off and go to DC, or the beach.

Because Brownie was never alone when she lived with the lady, she cannot be left alone now. She howls pitifully if I get in the car without her. 'She'll get used to it,' I thought the first time.

But upon returning, I found the house in disarray. A mad rumpus had occurred. Lamps were askew. My mahogany table had been gouged by a claw. A vase of flowers was overturned.

It's almost time for my vacation. Now, every dog's Auntie Margo needs an Auntie Margo of her own.

— December 2006

A Toddler in the House

I am one of those cartoon women. You know the ones. They're slapping their foreheads, proclaiming, "I can't believe I forgot to have children!"

The time and the stars and, yes, the man, never came into alignment. Time, which there always seemed to be an abundance of, marched on until it disappeared altogether. Much like the men. I was sorry to see the time go.

So now, I have a dog.

While I never had children, I think I now know what it might have been like. I believe that having little Brownie is a lot like having a toddler in the house.

I do know this: It must be easier to find a babysitter for a toddler, than for a dog. And really, what would be the more joyful and simple task: keeping a close eye on a dog, or a child?

Before I adopted her, Brownie lived with a sweet little old lady who never went anywhere. Brownie was never, ever alone. She spent four or five years living like this.

And then, she came to live with me. I am out and about much of the time. It is very fortunate for both of us that I work at home. Most offices frown on bringing your dog to work. (I think it would be a wonderful thing if more offices considered this policy. There would be far fewer grumpy workers. And customers would appreciate it, too. I know that if a shop has a cat or dog, I'll go in there just to see the pet. And then, I will almost always buy something.)

Somehow, although she had never ridden in a car in her life, Brownie took to it immediately. She sits quietly on her little blanket in the passenger seat. She's not tall enough to see out the window, but she is attuned to the sound of the turn signal. When I slow down and hit that blinker, she's up with her paws on the dashboard, peering to see what fabulous place we're going to grace with our presence. No matter where it is, she is hap-hap-happy.

In the beginning, I had a rule that I wouldn't go anywhere that would mean leaving Brownie home alone for more than two hours. Turns out, the first thing I learned is that it only takes her 10 minutes to find or create an escape route. Now that I've learned all those routes – after much angst and heartache and gratefulness to kind neighbors, not to mention construction and repair expense – I believe she is safely "trapped" inside when I leave the driveway.

I've now worked up to four hours of "away time." The one instance where I was gone for four hours and 15 minutes, there was carpet cleaning to do when I returned home.

Another way Brownie is much like a toddler is her eating habits. You know those cute pictures with a baby in a high chair, food all over her face and the tray and the floor? That is much like meal time in the Oxendine household.

Apparently, Brownie never had her food in a dish before she came here. She turns over the bowl and scatters crunchies across the floor. Then, she proceeds to snuffle around and delicately eat every single crunchy, one by one. After that, she goes into floor-monitor mode, eating everything she finds – an errant spinach leaf, a few grains of spilled rice, a dropped cashew, a speck of pants lint.

Like the best of toddlers, Brownie sleeps a lot. Her day, really, consists of eating, sleeping, piddling, walking with wide-eyed wonder, and bestowing ceaseless adoration upon me.

As I said, it's a lot like having a toddler in the house. Except I don't eventually have to pay for her college education.

— March 2009

I Encounter a Vicious Beast

It's been a week of cats and dogs.

You've read of my new-found adoration for those of the canine persuasion. And I've always loved cats, especially Chloe and even ZuZu, who are scrapping and snarling at each other as I write this.

I spent most of last week at my favorite getaway with my two favorite dogs. I've grown so attached to these dogs that I even dream of them. When I wake up, I have to go gaze at their photograph, as if they were a loved one lost at sea.

But every time I go to pet-sit, some weird mishap befalls me.

Thus it was that in the wee hours last Monday night, I got out of a strange bed and wandered down a strange hall, only to trip over a dark brown dog sleeping on a dark brown floor. I pitched forward with wild abandon, waking the slumbering dear, as I crashed to the floor.

I was certain I had broken my right arm. It hurt so much, I could do nothing but lie there and moan.

The dogs, now fully awake, rushed to give me succor. They placed themselves on either side of me and licked me so hard my hair was soaked. The one over whom I'd tripped whimpered in my ear. I could almost hear her cry, "I'm so sorry. I didn't know you were clumsy and blind. Please forgive me."

It's funny the thoughts that fly through your head as you take a fall. Mine were this: Cripes, the dog! I'm falling! I've broken my arm! Now I've got to call the rescue squad, but I can't remember where the phone is and it's 3 a.m. and the squad will take 40 minutes to get here and they'll see me in my pajamas!

All this in about a nanosecond.

Thank heavens, my right arm was not broken after all. The next night, I left the hall light burning bright.

As soon as one pet-sitting venture ended, the next began. I loaded up my considerable traveling togs and accoutrements from one strange house, and unloaded at another.

This time, I'd care for a single cat. No trouble at all, one would think. Cats don't have to be taken outside at midnight for a quick piddle; cats munch on a single little bowl of food throughout the day. They are independent creatures who require very little care. I wish I could take them for walks, but I've tried it and it is not a pleasant adventure.

So here I was, a gypsy in yet another palace. This particular palace had a fine attribute: A fireplace in the bedroom. 'I'm in heaven!' I thought. 'And naught to do but keep crunchies in a bowl and make a scoop through the litter box once a day.'

Along about the second day, I began to think this particular cat had no redeeming qualities. She is a most unsocial cat; when I entered the house, she sat there glowering at me, turned up her tiny pink nose and padded upstairs. I only saw her when crunchies clattered into the cat dish.

Saturday night, I'd been invited next door for dinner. Primped and perfumed, I sauntered to the front door, and encountered the cat. She did not seem inclined to let me pass.

"Hello there, Daisy," I cooed. "I've got to go out now, but I'll give you a tasty treat when I return."

I reached down to pat her head and things turned nasty. Very nasty. She yowled and screamed and lunged through the air at me, clamping her teeth into my right hand and drawing a surprising quantity blood. I, too, yowled and screamed. Never have I met such a vicious little beast!

I raced, bleeding, to the neighbors' house and entered the little dinner party with this opening line: "I need first aid!"

"I'll bet that cat bit you," the neighbor quickly surmised. "She is a vicious little beast. We don't go near her without wearing heavy gloves."

Now they tell me.

— February 2002

Max's Curious Adventure

We do not know what occurred during Max the Cat's 28-hour adventure.

Max – a recalcitrant and snarly sort, deeply doted upon by his "mother" – isn't talking.

That's a shame, really, because there are many questions I'd like Max to answer.

Here is what we do know: Max stealthily crept downstairs at 6 a.m. Monday, and swiftly darted outside when Auntie Margo, somewhat snarly herself, let out Sam the Wonder Dog.

We know that, after Auntie Margo went to work and a scary electrical storm moved in, workmen outside saw a black streak barreling toward the house. We know that no one thought to let the cat inside at that time.

We know that several terrific thunderstorms, with drenching rain, occurred throughout the day. We know that, when Auntie Margo returned from work, Max was nowhere to be found.

We know the poor auntie called until she was hoarse. We know she turned on every porch light, and hollered at every door. We know that she used not only the name "Max," but also "Punkin' Pie," which is the doting mother's pet name for the grumpy, disobedient pet. We know that at midnight, when she could finally stay awake no longer, Auntie Margo made one last round of the outside doors, affecting what she considered a darn good imitation of Max's mother's voice.

Did we mention that Auntie Margo actually called the construction workmen at their homes to discern whether they had seen the cat?

We know she went to bed worried. She left the windows open, in case she heard a plaintive cry in the night. Her slippers were at the ready, so she could stumble through the strange, dark house and welcome, with open arms, the pitiful, drenched creature.

We know that, when she awoke at 6 a.m. after a fitful, fretful night, the first thing Auntie Margo did was run to the window and call the cat's name. Before she even brushed her teeth, she went downstairs and checked all the doors.

We know that, as she made her coffee, she imagined the sneaky cat lying charred and sodden, having been struck by lightning during his happy adventure. We also know that she imagined killing the cat herself, should he ever reappear.

We know Auntie Margo gazed with some sadness at a ball of string near the coffeemaker. She had been advised to use it to lure Max inside, should he go out and want to stay there. She thought to herself, Ha! If I could see him to use the string ploy, I wouldn't need the string. We know that Auntie Margo secretly envisioned using the string for a different purpose, should the cat ever reappear.

Auntie Margo was aware that, before much more time passed, she would be duty-bound to call the doting mother – one of her best friends – and reveal the upsetting news. She hoped this news would not include mention of charred fur, or tearful inquiries about burial sites.

After Max had been missing for 27 hours and 45 minutes, Auntie Margo had to get ready for another day of work. While in the shower, though, a thought struck her: She had neglected to call upon the singular entity who could find the missing cat.

We know that a hasty, heartfelt plea went to Saint Francis, patron saint of animals, asking for his assistance. "Please bring him home, the sooner the better!"

We know that, 10 minutes later, the cat strolled in the side door, affecting a macho attitude. We know that he was uncharred and, indeed, quite dry. We know that the only sign of a 28-hour outdoor adventure was a single tiny pine needle, clinging to his sleek, black fur.

We know that Auntie Margo is considering giving up this pet-sitting nonsense.

— June 2005

Swimming with the Fishes

It's summertime and it's blistering hot and all I can think of is getting in the water. And staying there.

I'm a "water baby." I learned to swim early – well, for the 1950s, it was early – around age three. I've nearly drowned twice, that I know of; heaven knows how many times I blithely swam, unaware of imminent danger.

I did most of my swimming in the Florida Keys and the Caribbean. I've swam in the Atlantic, the Pacific, the Aegean and the Mediterranean. I yearn to swim in the Ionian Sea, and am determined I will, one day. You can keep the Baltic and the North seas, thank you.

My most memorable beautiful sight while swimming happened in the Gulfstream as the sun was setting one August evening. We were out in the boat and, as always, relished a dip with snorkels and fins. Unless you're wading, it's never a good idea to be without snorkel, mask and fins in any ocean or sea. You need to see what else is there. You may need to get away from it fast, without much splashing.

That night, in the last rays of sunlight, we surprised two leopard rays nestling on the bottom. Their wing spans were six and eight feet, and they were a most magnificent, almost spiritual sight.

I've always wanted to swim with the whales, but have never had the opportunity. If I ever do, I am in there! If I don't get killed, I'll remember it the rest of my life. If I do die, well, what a wonderful way to go.

While diving for treasure and swimming for sport in the Keys, I adapted an odd but security-minded technique: Mask, fins and snorkel a must. Free-dive below the surface, glide with as little movement as possible, swim in big circles so you can survey the surrounds. Dangerous fish like to lurk. You need to know they're there. Never wear jewelry; wear a suit that matches the sea. Sharks have poor eyesight, but they love the sparkling flash of earrings. Their favorite color? International orange, the same color as your life vest.

Back in Key West, about all we ate was fish and Florida lobster we'd caught ourselves. We didn't catch them so much as spear them. I never could bring myself to do that so, since everyone had a job, mine became swimming the speared fish back to the boat. It was a most dangerous job: Haul a wriggling, bleeding, frightened fish on the end of spear, hundreds of yards back to the boat. Here's the technique I adopted: Swim about six feet below the surface; hold the wriggling, bleeding fish on the spear completely out of the water, so it attracts as few predators as possible. Sure, if anyone were looking, it would be a remarkable sight – an impaled fish making its way through a seemingly empty sea. When you get near the boat, pitch the fish and spear into it. Then, scramble as quickly as you can over the transom and out of the water.

Despite precautions, I'd often attract packs of curious barracuda while doing this. Barracuda never stop gnashing their razor-toothed jaws. They are like a pack of wild, hungry dogs. The way to deal with them is to be scary yourself. This requires fortitude and fearlessness: I always carried a broomstick with a nail on it in my other hand; lunge at the barracuda pack underwater; shout at them through your snorkel; they will usually disperse.

These days, I spend my water time at The Gristmill pool or tubing on the Jackson River. There's little danger lurking; there's little need for fearlessness; nothing I can think of wants to eat me. Sure, there's less excitement, but I'm older now. I can live with that.

— July 2001

Dallying with the Dolphins

Sunday morning, National Public Radio bestowed upon me the, dare we say, "thrust," of this week's column: Dolphins.

No, not the Miami Dolphins; rather, the dolphins that swim off the Miami shore, and other oceans of the world.

What piqued my interest was a brief bit about "Georges," a dolphin of no little fame off the coast of Dorset, England.

Swimmers, especially those of the female persuasion, are being warned to stay out of the sea. It seems that Georges, who weighs about 400 pounds, is seeking a mate. Trolling the sandbars, if you will. Looking for love.

Dolphins, you may know, are some of this planet's most intelligent mammals. Their brains, by the way, are even larger than those of humans. Perhaps dolphins are THE smartest mammal, and we're just not smart enough to realize it!

"Georges" – a French name, wouldn't you know – is apparently lurking in the shallows and foisting his amorous attentions upon female swimmers. According to the NPR report, "He won't take 'no' for an answer."

Hmmm.

One female pundit on the show opined, "Maybe the Dorset tourism bureau should use this as a promotion, rather than a warning."

Imagine. A host of lonely female tourists, flocking to Dorset, thong bikinis in hand, to seek the attentions of an intelligent, 400-pound Frenchman who won't take "no" for an answer. It could be England's answer to the Cote d'Azur.

I've always wanted to visit the English coast. Perhaps now I'll forego the Cotswolds for the action along the Dorset shore. Who knows what sights I might see!

I have actually been swimming with dolphins. None of them, to my knowledge, had romantic intentions. They did, however, seem quite friendly. They smiled a lot. A few even winked at me, I swear. They have smooth, muscled gray flanks. They are prone to good-natured nudging. They seem to enjoy a good joke among themselves, always chuckling.

Now, I am led to wonder just what all the chatter was about.

Flipper: "Hey, this one seems approachable."

Winky: "Yeah, and check out that pink bikini. Think she's looking for love?"

Georges: "Oui, but in all ze wrong places!"

(The dolphins chuckle good-naturedly at Georges's bon mot.)

When I was working for Treasure Salvors, we had a "pet" of sorts at the wreck site, about 40 miles out to sea. His name was Ralph. He was a barracuda.

Ralph was about six feet long, which is pretty hefty for that species. And if there could ever be such a thing as a benign barracuda, it was Ralph. He would hang out with us while we combed the seabed for gold, silver, emeralds or, more likely, pottery shards.

As the days, weeks and months wore on, Ralph grew larger. He seemed measure about eight feet the last time I saw him. Then again, anything seems larger underwater.

It's no wonder Ralph kept growing. He'd feast nightly on the garbage the guys threw overboard after dinner.

Garbage, we figured, was biodegradable. Turns out, Ralph glommed up the garbage before it ever had a chance to biodegrade.

Little did we know, Ralph wasn't the only scavenger circling our boat every night. One morning we caught a 16-foot tiger shark. After we hung him upside down, portions of our dinners for the last week spilled onto the deck. So did a license plate from Mississippi. And a four-foot black-tip shark, minus the head. And a fisherman's yellow slicker with a giant piece missing. Uh oh.

After we each had our photo taken alongside the grinning dead beast, every one of us came up with a reason why we couldn't dive that day. Earaches. Sinus problems. Pressing business back on shore.

The old Mafia adage notwithstanding, I'd give anything to swim with the fishes again. Perhaps a trip to merry England is in order.

— June 2002

Wherein I Ride an Elephant

In a rural locale, one's opportunities to ride an elephant are few and far between.

Back when I was a reporter, all sorts of oddball opportunities presented themselves. By far, the most unusual experience was riding an elephant in Warm Springs. Our community radio station was bringing the circus to town. The station manager mentioned during an interview that he was looking for "two lucky local celebrities" to ride an elephant into the ring at the start of the show. "Oh wow! Please, tell me I can do it!" I gushed.

"You mean you'd actually want to?" he asked, somewhat skeptical.

"I'd love to do it! I'd pay money to do it!"

"All righty then; that was easy," he said, seeming surprised. Turns out, he'd been wracking his brain to come up with someone foolhardy, reckless, and known to all. And there I was, pleading for the chance.

After some cajoling, a county supervisor who also sat on the radio board agreed, too. I imagined the supervisor and the reporter, smiling bravely, perched precariously atop a plodding pachyderm. I imagined who among our many detractors might be in the crowd of spectators. "Better make sure it's a bullet-proof elephant," I joked. The station manager did not laugh.

The Big Day dawned dark and dank, with a drenching downpour. This, I thought, is not the day to climb aboard a rain-slicked circus elephant.

But I persevered, entering the tent "backstage," past camels, ponies who could count, and man-eating tigers. I gave my name to a rather glamorous blonde clad in a sparkly gown, blue high heels and an old white bathrobe.

"I'm riding the elephant!" I announced.

She looked me over with a cool eye. "We already have two people riding," she said, turning away.

My heart sank.

"Who are they?" I demanded.

"The beauty queen and the supervisor."

Sounded like a fractured fairy tale. Or a late-night cable movie.

"Can't three of us ride?" I pleaded.

"No one wants to ride an elephant in this weather," the cool blonde replied. "You'll get wet."

I sidled over to Angela, the beauty queen. She wore her sparkling tiara, jeans, a white sweater, and clogs with no socks.

"You'll get pretty wet riding that elephant," I noted, in a manipulative manner. While she mulled that over, the supervisor appeared and, in a gentlemanly fashion, volunteered to let Angela and me share the spotlight.

The circus master, in a rain-soaked yellow slicker and big Australian hat, led us outside to some metal stairs. Towering placidly on the other side was one huge elephant. Two circus fellows held her, shaking their heads and laughing at us.

"What's the elephant's name?" I shouted.

"Okah," they hollered, in the deafening rain.

"Oprah?"

"No, Okah."

"Okra?"

"O-K-A-H!"

"Oh. OK."

"No. Okah!"

That settled, Angela and I clambered aboard and sat astride a sodden old rug, straddling the swaying, four-ton behemoth. Okah was none too mindful of personal hygiene. Her hair sprouted willy-nilly in coarse, lonely wisps. She had spent the afternoon picking up hay with her elastic trunk, and gaily tossing it over her head. It stuck there, a natural adornment of sorts. She cast one giant eye over her massive shoulder at us and … we were off! I was not prepared for her swift, rolling gait. I was not prepared for the sheer height of it. I was not prepared for straddling the saturated rug in my new purple sweatpants. But off we went: Angela, in her once-perfect hairdo, twinkling tiara and fashionable clogs; I, in my soggy leisurewear, holding tight and screaming.

Okah knew just where she was going. This was fortuitous, since we were on our own; no knowledgeable handler led her on a leash, or even stood at the ready, should we take a tumble. We saw the tent entrance coming at us far too quickly and, it seemed, not nearly high enough to accommodate our height atop the elephant. "Duck!" I shouted.

We ducked. We popped back up again. The slickered-ringmaster made an announcement, but I doubt anyone heard it above the whooping laughter of the crowd. As he hollered "Margo Oxendine, newspaper reporter," Okah pirouetted on one foot, lifted her trunk, and emitted a loud, braying trumpet. It sounded like this: "Boooooooooooo!"

Cripes, I thought. Everyone's a critic.

— February 2003

Say hay!

Say hay!

I know it should be "say hey," but hay is what's on my mind.

Right now I am being paid to do something I would have paid my whole allowance for in childhood: feed horses.

I couldn't get enough of horses as a girl. I couldn't snuggle in close enough, couldn't nuzzle their exquisitely soft noses enough, couldn't save enough to buy and then feed one of my own.

In California, I took riding lessons, and even showed for awhile. Then tragedy struck, in the form of a bad fall that took a near-fatal toll. After $60,000 worth of surgery, I wasn't too keen on snuggling and nuzzling any more horses.

Now, I'm bravely tramping out into a field of hungry horses on the loose. I know a horse can sense fear, so I make sure I'm armed with bravado and a fistful of carrots. I'm hoping the aroma of the carrots will cover any whiff of fear.

Breaking up and putting out bales of hay for horses is new to me. Here are the first two things I learned: It's dirty work, and it plays hell with a manicure. After three days, though, I'm learning something else: It's fun, even if I do get a little dirty.

Enjoying getting dirty is certainly a first for me. The whole task makes me feel somehow powerful. Who knew?

I give each massive steed a tiny handful of grain in their stall. Then, I scurry out to the hay barn, break a bale in half, load it into an odd little cart, and head to the field. There, I fluff the sweet, precisely-compressed hay (how do they do that?) into ten perfect little piles. By the time I'm on my third pile, the horses are heading toward me at a brisk clip. Thank heavens, they stop when they reach a pile of hay. I then move on, quickly, laying out the remaining seven piles. It's like the old game, "beat the clock," but I call it "beat the clop."

Laying out the hay this morning reminded me of an odd day at the circus in San Francisco. My mate decided to plant a tiny garden in the miniscule backyard of our city flat. He'd heard that elephant dung made great fertilizer. Ringling Brothers was in town, so we set out to the circus to collect some "zoo doo."

This was long before zoo doo was trendy. The circus people thought we were daft when we explained our mission. Nonetheless, they pointed us toward the elephant corral, and urged us to help ourselves.

We had black garbage bags and a shovel. I got to hold the bag, while he shoveled in the doo. It was a perfect metaphor for our relationship.

Out of the corner of my eye, movement occurred. I glanced up, and saw a parade of elephants passing silently just 10 feet from us. They were wearing gaily-colored tutus and tiny cocktail hats. They seemed to be smiling.

As we continued our task, carts carrying roaring tigers and lions passed close on the other side. Tom Thumb stepped out from his trailer, looked at us, and shook his head in disgust. A big brown bear was dancing in the background.

It was the most fun I've ever had at a circus.

Back on the freeway, our station wagon, laden with black plastic bags of clumpy material, was pulled over by the California Highway Patrol. They eyed our cargo suspiciously. Upon inspection, they shook their heads in distaste and let us pass.

The doo was carefully spread across our tiny garden plot. I guess fertilization occurred. I do know this: That summer we grew a marvelously healthy crop of hay.

— April 2005

Bee Very Afraid

Bomb-sniffing bees.

What will they think of next?

Driving home from work Monday, I chuckled over a report on National Public Radio. A very sincere scientist was boasting about bomb-sniffing bees.

I don't know who thought of the idea, or what possessed them to, but some research group – probably one with a nice, fat government grant – decided that bees are the next big buzz in bomb detection.

I don't know if anyone has yet informed the bees. Perhaps they're easily duped.

In my opinion, this does not bode well for travelers. We've not had an easy time of it lately, anyway. Personally, I'd much rather see a cute little beagle or a noble Labrador retriever snuffling toward my suitcase.

Imagine the havoc wreaked should a hive of 30,000 bomb-sniffing bees meet with some mishap on the baggage carousel.

It does, however, give a new meaning to the phrase "sting operation."

Whenever I hear of bees, I think of one fateful morning in sunny Key West.

I was sipping Cuban coffee at my kitchen table, looking out the window, when what should walk past but a fellow in a beekeeper's outfit. He tottered under the weight of five or six boxes of bees.

He was heading toward my backyard.

"Hey!" I hollered. "What are you doing out there?"

"I'm moving in," he called back, through the veil on his face. "Name's Leonard."

This was one of those big old Key West Victorians, converted into four apartments, one of which was mine. Another, apparently, was soon to be Leonard's.

My friend Tom, sharing coffee, decided to investigate matters in the backyard.

Tom was a six-foot-five-inch freckled Adonis, with a mass of curly, bright red hair. He strode up to Leonard, flip-flops flapping. Tom towered about a foot above him. That wasn't counting the four-foot tower of hives Leonard was toting.

Tom soon discovered Leonard had lots more hives in his truck. And he planned to set up his little bee town about eight feet from my clothesline.

Words were exchanged. Male posturing ensued, during which Leonard, stepping back from the angry redhead in his path, dropped the hives.

I watched all this from my window. It was an awesome sight to see.

The hives toppled to the ground, upsetting perhaps 100,000 (who was counting?) bees into the balmy morning air. The buzzing grew to a roar to rival a DC-10, as the bees became even more angry and confused.

It wasn't long before a Key West police cruiser pulled up in front of the house, its siren barely audible above the buzzing maelstrom of maddened bees.

Leonard, the only person properly clad for the occasion, waved his gloved hands in a gesture of surrender.

Tom engaged in a volatile battle with the bees. He swatted about madly, as the bees mistook his bright red hair for some sort of big, lovely flower.

The two policemen, both of Cuban descent, drew their guns and began hollering en Espanol. One exchanged his pistol for his nightstick and began batting at the bees. They refused to be subdued.

It's funny, but I do not recall the outcome of this beekeeping caper. I do know that I began hauling my wet laundry up the block, rather than venture out to my busy clothesline. The laundromat was not a pleasant place; a contingent of homeless "snowbirds" from up North considered it their private vacation hideaway.

Leonard's promise of free honey did little to persuade me from moving from 316 Elizabeth Street. My new little Conch cottage, which one had to hunker under an arch of banana trees to reach, was just six blocks away.

It was not an easy move. I owned little, but what little I owned did not include a car. Thus, the move was accomplished by countless trips with my belongings in a bicycle basket. I pedaled quickly, to escape an ominous buzzing in my ears.

— May 2002

Regrets: I have a few

I have no idea why I am sitting here this morning thinking about regrets.

Well, yes I do: I just saw the word "grumpy." I thought of myself. And then, I thought of one of my great regrets.

I'm sure we each have a list of Life's Big Regrets. Here are some of mine.

As a teen, I regret that I did not accept the full scholarship offered by Hollins University. What was I thinking? Remember, I was a teenager. I was convinced that I did not, and could never, have the wardrobe necessary to fit in with the other girls. Geez! Had I only known that, the fall I started college – at VCU, where wardrobes didn't matter – there would be a sudden and dramatic shift in fashion. Goodbye, Peter Pan collars, A-line skirts, Weejuns in every color. Hello, jeans and sneakers.

I regret that I chose theater as my major, rather than journalism.

I certainly have no regrets about traipsing off to Key West when I was 23. That flighty decision (Daddy's words, of course) turned into one of life's big adventures. My second day there, I met Mel Fisher and decided I wanted to dive for sunken Spanish treasure.

But working for Treasure Salvors eventually led to my greatest regret. Mel couldn't pay us in cash most of the time, so we got pieces of eight (silver Spanish coins), which we could then trade at Fausto's Groceria for Cuban coffee and bread. That was all we needed, anyway, since we had "the supermarket," that spot on the reef where grouper, yellowtail and Florida lobster hung out, just waiting to become dinner.

Mel also "paid" us with Treasure Salvors stock certificates. They were worthless at the time, really; still, we stockpiled them like they were checks that might be "good" someday.

After we found nine bronze cannons from the 1622 "Atocha" wreck, and lots of other gold and silver booty; after we went to Washington, DC and presented a cannon to Queen Sofia of Spain; after seven years of the laid-back, hedonistic Key West life, I started thinking about moving to San Francisco. By then, doing comedy had moved to the forefront of my life.

I sold my Treasure Salvors stock to a tourist on Duval Street one night. I do not recall his name. He may have been from Pennsylvania. He paid $3 a share for it. All the other divers were astounded at this windfall: "Margo got $3 a share from some tourist on the street!" No one had ever actually sold their stock for cash. Wasn't I the smart one?

Six weeks later, I was listening to the news in my San Francisco apartment, and learned that Treasure Salvors had discovered "the big pile" – the bulk of Atocha treasure we always knew was out there on the ocean floor. I called my friends. They were selling their stock to tourists for $300 a share.

Ah, regrets.

I was a comedian by then, though. With that came my next great regret. I really, really regretted it the morning I learned Richard Pryor had set himself ablaze while doing drugs. I was in Beverley Hills that morning, because I had a wonderful "gig" on tap: I was to "open" for Richard Pryor that night. I would have been paid $800 for 10 minutes of comedy.

Time for another career curve. I managed to find myself writing something other than comedy for a living. I managed to find myself back in Virginia, working for The Recorder newspaper. And, I had somehow managed to win a first-place national award for investigative reporting. The "big do" where the awards were handed out was at Disney World.

I took my mother (Daddy was, sadly, gone by that time – I know he would have been proud, at last!) and off we jetted to Orlando. There was a big party for us that night. And thinking about that party always brings to mind one of my greatest regrets. Snow White and the Seven Dwarfs were roaming about the party, posing for photos with us. I took a picture of Mom with Doc. But I failed to get a photo of myself with Grumpy.

Ah, life's big regrets.

— July 2008

Whistle While You Work

Despite numerous and noisy distractions, there's something to be learned about construction.

Especially when it's going on all around you.

I try to avoid housesitting when there's construction going on; yet, I sure don't blame the homeowners for wanting to skip out of town.

I've managed to avoid it for several years, but this week, I'm in the thick of a massive renovation and building project.

The first thing I've learned is, it's actually quite nice to get up at 6 a.m. The air is cool, morning fog lies in little pockets, all is peaceful and quiet.

That changes abruptly at 7 a.m., when the workmen arrive. Construction crews are probably the most prompt of all workers. At 7 on the dot, they're here – hailing one another with robust greetings, grinding, sawing, hammering, drinking coffee from giant thermal mugs.

And so the day begins.

They keep up a constant chatter, often shouting to be heard over the din of drills and compressors. There's a big, earth-moving sort of machine parked in the driveway right now. I hope to be gone when that thing roars into action.

Here's another thing I've learned: Construction crews are excellent mathematicians. All morning, I've listened to them doing complicated fractional math in their heads. They call out things like, "It's 24 and 3/8 on a three by 12 with seven-sixteenths joists." Or something like that.

I swear this morning I heard them talking about "toe jam" as something they were anxious to install on the wall.

In this project, they're making a garage into an expansive guest suite, and then building another new garage. Three cars will probably fit in there, along with a couple of motorcycles, a lawn tractor, and a snowplow. I believe it's larger than my home. Let's call it "The Garage Mahal."

Inside, they've rerouted an upstairs bathroom, and created a giant walk-in closet where, in truth, a dance could be held.

I've learned that construction workers love to sing. Loudly. And often. It's endearing, really, once one gets used to it. I've also learned that these fellows are quite adept at the knack of whistling. This truly seems to be the happiest of work sites. Have you ever entered an accounting firm, or a bank, and heard the workers whistling and singing?

This particular crew at this particular house is not all that bad, actually.

I've had, you see, my "trial by fire" with this situation. Years ago, I was blindsided by the construction crews. I didn't realize they were coming until they were there – all 19 of them. They rolled in with a shout and a roar. As I peered cautiously from behind the curtain upstairs, I saw one stripping to his underwear in the driveway. Then, he stepped into camouflage clothes, picked up a gun, and wandered into the woods.

I wonder, was he on the clock while hunting?

More than a couple of this crew looked as if they were on parole. Or perhaps not; I didn't check the radio for reports of prison escapes. I was afraid to make any noise at all. I cowered upstairs all day, waiting for them to leave at 5 p.m.

But that hour came and went, and still they stayed. They did not leave until dark, which was about 9 p.m.

Why, I wondered, do construction crews have to be so danged conscientious? Why couldn't they take a tip from postal workers, and shut down at the stroke of four? It would be a good idea for me to establish a friendly, accommodating relationship with the Garage Mahal crew. Come November, they'll be whistling at my place for the better part of the winter.

— June 2005

A Letter From My Contractor

I've just had some renovations done by a quiet, timely contractor.

Perhaps you are ready to hire a contractor of your own. Or soon will be. Choosing a contractor can be tricky. It would be helpful if, before we make that important decision, we had some idea whether our dream project might become a nightmare.

Here is a letter I wish I'd received from a previous contractor, before that job began ...

"Welcome to the world of homeowners who want to have a little work done. We hope you are in no hurry! We know you've pondered your various projects and priorities; what might cost more than you can imagine, what might inconvenience you the least.

"We know your project is important to you; it is important to us, too. Sort of.

"After you've made your decision, the first thing you should do is attempt to get a contractor to return your call. The adventure begins!

"During the estimate phase of the project, be sure to inquire about the amount of time the job might take, in addition to a 'ballpark' figure as to cost. And please, remember just how far we are from the nearest ballpark.

"Also be advised that, after the initial estimate, you may never actually see your contractor. That's what hourly workers are for, don't you know.

"Please understand that having us in your home might be a little scary. Some of us will, no doubt, be on parole. Others may appear to have recently escaped incarceration. You may be hesitant to leave us here alone; you may be hesitant to be alone here with us. This is called a conundrum.

"It is not unusual for a job estimated to take 'a half-day, maybe a day,' to easily take four or five weeks. Possibly more. Additionally, please be advised that your project may be an 'after-hours' affair. This should become apparent when, after seeing no workers on the job throughout the day, you hear buzz saws at 9:17 p.m.

"We understand your project – making a door where once there was a window – is, in your eyes, a simple enough task for contracting professionals. Remember, though, that 'professionals' is a subjective word.

"Please know that, just because you leave a note asking us to make sure the doors to the interior of the house are shut, while that gaping hole to the outside blows in snow and freezing wind, this probably will not happen. This should become quite clear as soon as your next heating bill arrives.

"You will perhaps be surprised to learn, after day four of the half-day job, that your door has been installed. Upside down. We hope you will find this amusing.

"By the way, it is our sincerest hope that your musical tastes run to heavy metal, bluegrass, or hip-hop music. We will bring our own boom boxes to the site, and serenade you with a constant barrage of such selections throughout the day. It is important that our crew be kept happy.

"During the course of our work, we may find it necessary to move a heat register in the room. It could take three weeks before we thoughtfully place the new register in the middle of the floor. During this time, the massive duct from the furnace will be left open in the basement. However, if you will simply make your concern about this known, our professional staff will stuff an old bath towel into the duct. Problem solved!

"Pay no mind to crumpled wrappers, empty bottles and cigarette butts scattered about your yard. They will complement the scraps of wood and vinyl siding, and the abandoned power tools strewn there. What better sign that progress is being made?

"You might not complain, because you'll perhaps be feeling rather hopeless and helpless about this project after a while, but we want to mention the grimy hand and fingerprints we will leave on the creamy bisque walls in our workroom. Do not attempt to wash these off. The only solution will be to have the entire room repainted. Should you desire, our staff of professionals will be happy to make an educated guess about the amount of time this new project might take and, of course, give you a 'ballpark' estimate of the cost."

Had I received this letter, valuable information would have been revealed. As for my fabulous new contractor, well, I refuse to reveal his name.

— October 2008

Selling Country Property

At the age of 12, I received what I thought was an odd and useless gift.

An elderly couple, the Pamplins, were friends of my parents. Stanley Pamplin was British, smoked a pipe, and wore the requisite tattered vest of good quality.

He knew I loved to read, so for Christmas that year, he gave me a book.

The title was Buying Country Property.

While I have just about every book I've ever owned – probably a thousand or so – I can't seem to put my hands on this one. I recall seeing it just a few years ago. I've combed through my collection for the past six hours, and it's nowhere to be found. I did find my 1962 copy of Auntie Mame, which I've probably read about five times.

But no Buying Country Property.

It's funny, because a book I thought was odd and useless at the time is one I'd love to read right now.

It turns out, Mr. Pamplin's gift was portentous.

I am now attempting to sell country property.

And, while I'm sure a book about real estate, written some 40 years ago, would be rather laughable today ("It is unadvisable to pay more than $200 per acre of country property," for instance), it could be helpful, still the same.

I added real estate to my several other ventures because I figured it would be quick, easy money.

Ha!

As is often the case, the joke's on me. In the past year, I've learned that real estate agents earn every cent. Provided they earn anything at all.

I was reminded of Mr. Pamplin's book just yesterday.

For the second time in a week, clients wanted to see some undeveloped property. As is the case with much rural land, property lines are vague. The most recent survey occurred in 1957.

For two weekends now, I've tramped through briars and brambles, across rocks and streams. The temperature has been in the 90s. It is the season for gnats. And thorns. And snakes.

While my clients are fit and spry, I fall short in these categories.

While my clients can be considered "outdoorsy," I cannot.

Since childhood, I have loathed getting dirty.

Yesterday was quite the experience.

In the midst of wandering through the forest, swatting gnats and keeping a close eye on the ground for slithery things with diamonds on their backs, an added adventure involved crawling through barbed wire.

I almost gave up halfway through this ordeal.

Straddling the old fence, with shaky rocks for a foothold, I realized my legs were too short and my pants were too flimsy. I wore a pair of sneaker-clogs. This is a nice fashion choice, unless one is traipsing through the forest.

Trapped between the rocks and the barbed wire, I was rethinking this particular career decision.

"Just put your hands on the ground and crawl through," my client urged.

I couldn't bring myself to say what I was thinking: "But, I'll get dirty!"

Later that afternoon, as the sweat dried and my blood pressure attempted to return to normal, I sat reading in my chair.

Ah, I sighed, this is my idea of activity.

I glanced down and saw a sight heretofore never seen: dirt under my fingernails.

That nasty problem taken care of, I settled back with my book.

I scratched my head.

I felt something there.

I carefully extracted what appeared to be a mouse turd.

Huh?

I felt around more carefully, and discovered yet another.

I have no earthly idea how mouse turds ended up in my hair, and I don't really want to know. My best guess is that, as I ducked under tree limbs and fought my way through thorny bushes, some tiny creature above me seized the opportunity for some jolly fun.

Life, as they say, is one big learning adventure.

Here's what I learned yesterday: When tramping through the woods, a scarf is a good idea. Also, it's best to forgo the Chanel No. 5 and spritz yourself with DEET instead.

I do not own jeans or hiking boots, but I think they would be a wise purchase, if I'm going to continue trying to sell country property.

If I could only find Mr. Pamplin's book, there are probably more helpful suggestions.

But maybe I'll just read Auntie Mame again.

— August 2006

The Mystery of the Missing Nuggets

I just spent a week with two comics.

No, not those loathsome lunks who vie to be the last one standing.

These comics were actually funny. Without even trying.

I've mentioned Brisco the Rhodesian Ridgeback before. He's the one who wolfed down a prime rib roast when I turned my back for two minutes.

Rhodesian Ridgebacks were bred, centuries ago, as lion hunters.

While I doubt that Brisco has ever seen a lion, he is quite adept at terrorizing squirrels and chipmunks.

Every morning at the crack of dawn, Brisco brays to be let outside.

Brisco does not bark. He brays. Like a donkey. It's quite disconcerting, as if a turkey bone is caught in his throat. For all I know, he may well have snarfed down a turkey while making his forays through the woods. But I think Brisco just likes to have his own distinctive voice. I've nicknamed him "Donkey Boy." He answers to that.

So, every morning when Donkey Boy brays at the door, I let him outside.

And, every morning, there is a fat, furry squirrel lurking on the doorstep. The dog and the squirrel take off at a frantic pace. I watch them until they're lost among the trees.

Apparently, this is a game they both enjoy. The very same squirrel waits patiently every morning. And if Brisco, who runs as fast as a cheetah, wanted to have this squirrel for breakfast, I'm sure he would have done so, long ago.

Donkey Boy has another odd trait: He sleeps with one eye open. This, too, can be disconcerting. It's difficult to grouch at a snoring dog to "Quiet down!" if, when you look at him, he appears to be staring back at you.

I guess this should come as no surprise. If a dog is bred to hunt lions, he would be wise to sleep with at least one eye open.

Since the missing roast incident, I've learned that Brisco has a reputation for such things. It is a prized anecdote of family lore that, one day when everybody returned from a baptism at church, half the christening cake was missing. Brisco looked quite innocent lying there on the rug. He did not confess when everyone blamed Dad. It was only when someone noticed pink icing on his whiskers that the true culprit was revealed.

And then there's Max the cat. Max is quite the largest feline I've ever seen, weighing in at a hefty 23 pounds. When Max lies down, the spread is more than a foot across.

Max is, as one would expect, on a diet. This makes him grumpy. I can relate.

Each morning and evening, I am to put exactly one-eighth of a cup of nuggets in Max's dish. That amounts to eight little nuggets, about what would fill a coffee scoop.

Max lives for his eight nuggies. It is almost impossible to put them in his dish, because his massive furry head is already poised over it. When the nuggies appear, Max lies flat on the floor, wraps his paws around the dish, and eats them one by one. His purr can be heard a room away.

At anytime during the day, when one heads toward the kitchen, Max is there. He yowls piteously and galumphs toward his dish, glancing over his shoulder. He looks quite hopeful. If no nuggets are forthcoming, Max will sit and stare menacingly at the offending party.

There was a mystery afoot during my recent stay. It was quite curious. Every day when I cleaned Max's litter box, there was no evidence of the recycled nuggets. And then I noticed Brisco, the dog who indeed eats anything, watching me. He had one eye open. He looked quite innocent.

I think the mystery is solved.

— January 2005

I Learn to Play Ball

I learned something new this week.

I learned how to play ball. And love it.

Just two weeks ago, I mentioned how I'd never learned to play ball games. I was always the last one chosen for any team. Ah, I whined, woe is I.

I'm not whining any more. I'm whooping with glee.

The fellow who taught me how to play ball and love it is Puerto Rican by birth. He has silky white hair, and red freckles. He has large, luminous brown eyes. He has a lovely smile, and the whitest teeth I've ever seen.

I'm in love with him. We're already sleeping together.

He stands about 18 inches tall at the shoulder, and one of his toes is pink.

His name is Carlito and, if you haven't guessed by now, he's a dog.

Details are sketchy, but apparently Carlito was homeless, roaming the streets of Puerto Rico, when he was discovered by a beautiful blonde woman. Somehow, she pulled all the strings necessary to fly him back to Fort Lauderdale.

Today, he enjoys the lap of luxury many of us could only hope for: A place on the ocean in Florida, and a lush home in the mountains of Virginia. Here, he lives in my idea of the perfect "exclusive community": Children are scarce, and dogs are welcome.

Carlito's savior had to hie back to Florida to prepare for yet another hurricane last week. I'd promised myself I wouldn't add any new dogs to the "Auntie Margo" mix but, well, I'm just a girl who can't say no. So, I moved into Carlito's place.

Carlito has more toys than most two-year-old humans. He keeps them in a big basket, and searches through it several times a day for something amusing. I laugh out loud at his antics.

But more than anything, Carlito likes to play ball. The ritual is this: A raggy old tennis ball is thrown from the deck into the woods. Carlito bounds after it, brings it back, drops it at your feet, and the game is repeated.

I was told to do this for five minutes, twice a day. I think we spent at least 90 minutes out there yesterday.

No matter where the ball goes, Carlito will find it. Quickly. I tried to trick him once, and threw the ball in a different direction from where he was headed. Before long, we were both out there, hunting for the soggy ball. A tennis ball is difficult to locate in a forest carpeted with greenish-gold fallen leaves.

I gave up and trooped back to the deck. Carlito came clicking along behind me, and bounced the ball at my feet.

One night, around the darkest hour, I let Carlito out for a quick piddle before bed. He joyfully returned with a tennis ball I'd never seen, and dropped it at my feet. I chuckled.

"OK, I'll throw it, but you won't find it in the dark," I told him.

He dashed into the night after the ball. He was gone for awhile. He returned, looking a little dejected.

"I said you couldn't find it in the dark," I told him. He looked at me with his big, brown eyes and then opened his mouth. The ball bounced onto the deck and rolled toward me. I swear, he was grinning.

I'm sure the neighbors wondered who was laughing so loudly, outside, at midnight.

It was I, gleefully embracing the idea that I'd finally found a ball game I liked. I'm sure that, if Captain Carlito were ever choosing a ball team, I'd be one of the first ones picked.

— October 2004

Jailbirds

No one has yet to ask me, Have you ever been in jail? The answer would be yes. Sort of.

Here's what happened. Way back when, my roommate and I met a couple of Duke guys, Corky and Biff, at a fraternity mixer. We made plans to go to a Three Dog Night concert the following weekend. Cindy and I would drive down from Virginia, and meet our North Carolina dates at a South Carolina campus.

My roommate Cindy was a statuesque blonde with green eyes and a very bright smile. She drove a red Corvette convertible.

So, very early that Saturday morning, we packed the Corvette and headed south. We had maybe $20 between us, yet not a worry in the world. Cindy, as was her manner, had rollers in her hair. I, as was my manner, was perfectly coifed.

Cindy did all the driving. I decided to sleep through North Carolina.

About mid-morning, Cindy's excited voice disturbed my doze.

"Wake up! There's roadblock ahead! There must be some criminals on the loose!"

I opened my eyes and saw lots of flashing lights and state police cars way down the interstate. I looked at the speedometer. I could not see the needle. I knew from experience, if I could not see that needle, we were going over 100 miles an hour.

"How fast are you going?"

She gave me a sheepish grin.

"About 145."

"Slow down," sighed I, the state trooper's daughter. "That roadblock is for us."

Police cars of many localities surrounded us. They looked grim.

Unperturbed, Cindy began pulling out curlers and fluffing her hair. She turned on the bright, blonde smile. I sat up straight, and checked my lipstick in the mirror.

We came to a screeching stop at the roadblock, and about 10 state and local police cars boxed us in. Officers alit from their cruisers, guns drawn, and approached. Oddly, they already knew Cindy's name.

"Reinhardt!" they bellowed. "Step out of the *#%# car!"

Chest out, stomach in, Cindy sensuously did just that.

"Do you have any idea how fast you were going?" one shouted.

"Well," she giggled girlishly. "I guess I was going a little fast."

"A little fast! We don't have a radar gun that can clock your speed! We've been trying to catch you for 20 miles!"

"I guess I'm gonna get a ticket," she said, green eyes downcast.

"A ticket? You're going to jail, young lady!"

"What about me?" I asked innocently.

"You're going right along with her."

I thought about invoking my well-known Virginia trooper father and then, smartly, thought better of it.

They gave us a police escort into the town of Kannapolis. People along the sidewalks stopped to stare; I crawled up on the seat top of the bright red convertible and waved like a beauty queen.

First, we saw a grumpy judge. He made reference to "scraping you two up off the highway," and then imposed a fine of hundreds of dollars.

"I'll have to call my parents," Cindy said. I offered no such thing.

"You can both wait in jail until the money gets here," said the judge.

The jailers had no idea what to do with us; their cells were filled with scummy-looking real criminals. They decided to let us wait in their "lobby." The TV was on; we found a dance show, and began to boogie. I inadvertently danced into the gumball globe, sending hundreds of gumballs spinning across the floor. The officers were not amused. They let us walk next door to get burgers; we discovered "the red Corvette girls" were town celebrities; our burgers were free.

When our bail arrived hours later, we got a police escort out of town and an order to never show our faces there again. They warned that every police car in North and South Carolina would be on the lookout for us.

Needless to say, we were late meeting our dates. Then we drove around the campus, unable to find the concert hall. Finally, we saw another car – a long black limousine. We pulled alongside.

"We're late for the Three Dog Night concert!" we called over. "Can you help us?"

"You think you're late?" they answered. "Follow us!"

They were, of course, Three Dog Night. They sat us up on the stage with them. It was more fun than jailbirds deserved.

— May 2001

"Those were the days, my friend"

It's August, the height of bikini season.

I remember the days when I owned, oh, probably at least a dozen bikinis. My very favorite was the satiny pale pink, followed closely by the hot pink with white polka dots. I think they were size four.

When my friend and I moved to Key West, we had one suitcase completely dedicated to bikinis. In Key West, a girl simply cannot own too many bikinis. We wore them with pride.

I recall a certain day. We put on our suits – me, the shiny pale pink; she, the oddly attractive green and blue one my mother handmade, complete with sarong. We hopped on our bikes and rode toward the beach. We stopped at The Fourth of July, a Cuban restaurant, to buy our two main food staples: Cuban bread and homemade sangria. Oh, those were the days, my friend.

We walked out of the restaurant and tires squealed, followed by a loud crash. We had not only stopped traffic, we'd caused an accident. The funny thing is, while loud shouting and blame-laying usually follows such incidents, the two fellows looked out their windows at us and hollered, "Wooo Hooo!" Or something like that.

Rather than feel complimented, we sighed as we climbed back on our bikes.

"Will there ever come a day," I grumbled, "when guys will stop whistling and hollering at us? I am sick and tired of it!"

I often thought, back then, "I can't wait till I'm old and fat and can walk down the street without creating a stir."

Those were the days, my friend. And they have come to an end.

I do not remember the last hoot or holler I garnered, other than, "Hey lady! Watch where you're going!"

Funny thing about our heydays. How often, in your youth, did you see a photograph of yourself, clad in a bikini or anything, really, and think, "Oh good heavens I'm fat."

Do you look back fondly on those photos today and chuckle? I do.

What did we really know, back then? By golly, we looked fabulous!

A fashion piece in the Associated Press recently bestowed these "Tips for Bikini Season." Perhaps you'll find them more helpful than I did.

"Don't worry if you forgot about bikini season," it begins. Well, I won't and I did.

"It's not too late to get ready for the big reveal." Oh yeah, it is.

One key hint here, as is always the case in a fashion piece, is, "Accessorize. Try a great pair of earrings, an anklet or belly ring, cool sunglasses, lovely flip flops." I do wear great earrings and lovely flip flops. They don't make anklets to fit me; I cannot imagine a belly ring; "cool" sunglasses do not come in trifocals.

"Make the suit fit. You should not get bulging from the straps or material." They're kidding, right? "The bottom should not be baggy." No danger there. "And, the bottom should contour with your rear without pinching or sagging." My rear has not been pinched in, lo, so many years. As for the sagging, well…

"Accept yourself. Stand in front of the mirror with your bathing suit on." I can be paid to do most anything; standing in front of a mirror in a swimsuit is not one of them. I no longer even own a full-length mirror.

"Focus on the features you like." My hair and nails are fabulous.

"Then, focus on what you will do in the suit." About twice a year, I do get into a swimsuit. It is not a bikini. The first thing I do is throw on a cool and lovely cover-up. It is not removed until the instant I go in the water.

Finally, "Get on track. Start exercising and eating right today for a two-pound weight loss in one week."

The way I figure it, there's a slim chance – pardon the pun – that, if I did this, I could fit into that shiny pale pink bikini about, oh, August 2017.

— August 2009

The Mishappetizer

Whenever a bunch of girlfriends gather, chatter soon enough turns to recipes.

This is when I smile vacantly and wander off somewhere, anywhere, else.

When plans were being made for a dozen of us to flock to the beach recently, one woman brightly suggested we could each bring an appetizer.

Everyone thought that was a superb idea. Everyone, that is, except me.

"Please, don't ask me to cook!" I whined. "Can't I bring liquor instead?"

They turned on me as one.

"Surely you can make something," they said, rolling their eyes.

"Well, I'll be coming from Washington, D.C., so I won't be able to cook," was my swift reply. I mentally wiped my brow, certain I'd yet again escaped the nerve-wracking chore.

"For heaven's sake, can't you just pick up some chips and dip?" retorted one particularly bossy babe.

Thankfully, one of the women was then bitten on the lip by a bee in her soda, and I never had to answer.

This little incident preyed on my mind for the next few weeks, and came crashing to the fore as I drove to the shore. I was arriving just in time for brunch; I was hungry, and empty-handed.

Thank heavens I'd figured out a way around this while in Washington. I'd bought little treats at the Spy Museum for everyone. I may not have food, but by golly, I had a purse full of lipstick pens!

After brunch, I made a foray to the supermarket. There, I'd pick up the ingredients for the one "party" thing I can make, a sort of puff-pastry and brie concoction.

The recipe requires little: a tin of pop-out crescent rolls, a small wheel of brie, some pecans, brown sugar and white grapes.

First obstacle: no brie in any of the 22 aisles of the Kitty Hawk supermarket. I did find goat cheese, oops, pardon me: chevre. Well, I thought, it's cheese and I love it; it'll work. Then, no pecans. I upgraded to macadamia and pine nuts. I had to buy two pounds of brown sugar, though I only needed about two tablespoons.

The girlfriends gathered around the bar in the kitchen as I prepared to create my offering. They made no effort to mask their curiosity: Margo is cooking!

I furrowed my brow and frowned in concentration. Some of Bath's best hostesses were eagle-eyeing my every move, and I was working from memory. I'd last prepared this dish about two years ago, and I'd made it up, then.

"What temperature should I preheat the oven?" one helpful friend asked.

"I've no idea," I replied. "Whatever you think's best."

The girlfriends raised eyebrows at one another over top of their margaritas. My theory of cooking is this: give guests enough to drink, and they won't care what you make.

At the last minute, I foraged through the fridge and found some pesto sauce. I was inspired to slather it on top of the goat cheese and pastry, just before baking. While the thing was in the oven, I sautéed the macadamia and pine nuts in brown sugar and butter, then poured it over the hot, puffy pastry. I threw on, oops, garnished the dish with white grapes and, voila, it was ready to serve.

I don't know whether it was the margaritas, the mandarin orange martinis that followed, or the fact that everyone was famished after a walk on the beach, but my happenstance appetizer was a huge hit with the ladies.

"This is the best thing I've ever tasted in my life!" gushed not one, but at least two of my friends. Perhaps they were just being polite, but considering how they wolfed it down, I don't think so.

— November 2003

I'm a Stranger Here

Arthur Frommer, who probably knows more about travel than anyone since, say, Magellan, includes in his Top 10 Travel Tips the fact that you should try to learn a little of the native language before you go.

I started five months ago, but it's still all Greek to me.

I've always had a knack for languages. But now I know why that "all Greek to me" bit is so popular. Not only are the words completely new, they're formed from an alphabet completely different from our own.

I'm still attempting to pronounce the letter x, or chi, properly, without sounding like Phyllis Diller with a phlegm problem.

That's why I bought the book, "Just Enough Greek," with a companion cassette. The couple speaking on the tape is Greek. I've listened at least 20 times and still cannot decipher their names. Their English is great – far better than my Greek – but it's not the English I hear every day in Bath County.

Listening to the tape in my car, I chuckled curiously whenever the woman repeated the phrase, "My husband has been stolen."

"Well," I would smirk to myself, "there's a phrase I certainly won't need."

Weeks passed before I discovered the stolen husband was actually a stolen handbag.

Now, this couple speaks so swiftly the whole pursuit seems rather a lost cause – a jumble of strange words and sounds that runs on so long your mind just glazes over, sort of like this sentence.

"Oh well," you tell yourself. "I don't think I'll need to ask anyone, 'Is this the road to the harbor?' If we're on a yacht, how can we miss the harbor?"

(Actually, when I got there, we nearly missed our so-called yacht; our cab driver could not find the harbor!)

The first word the couple on the tape teaches you to say is Love. The man uses it in this sentence: I prefer love.

I can't imagine saying that … or hearing it for that matter.

The second word they teach you is Help!

I decided to master that one. The very instant I sense danger, I am fully prepared to holler "Voithia!"

Just don't ask me to spell it.

One must wonder about visiting a country where a language tape teaches you how to shout "Help!" first thing.

And I hope I do not find myself desperately thumbing through the book to locate another phrase they provide, "I have been mugged."

I must also wonder why the phrase I consider most important, in any language, is not on the tape: "Where is the bathroom?"

I took it upon myself to learn that one regardless. It's easy to remember. The Greek word for "where" is "poo." Talk about a mnemonic device! I can now confidently inquire "Poo ena toilette?"

Of course, if they answer in Greek, I'm out of luck.

The book's pages are filled with phrases I don't believe I'll ever use. For instance, "I'm a stranger here."

Will I really need to explain that to anyone?

And how about, "It is the third of January, 1994."

Can't imagine using that, either.

"Please give me a call at 6:30 a.m."

Are you kidding?

"Would you rub suntan oil on my back?"

Naaah. Too risky. This is Greece, after all.

"Which is the best disco around here?"

I don't think so.

"Will she need an operation?"

God, I hope not.

"I don't have any money."

God, I hope not.

There is an entire section devoted to "Having a Drink." It includes such phrases as, "No ice, thanks," and "Another round of the same."

There is one phrase I find hilarious: "I'm absolutely knackered." I don't recall ever being absolutely knackered. But I am absolutely certain that, if I were, I would not be able to utter, "Ime ptoma stin koorassi."

(Hmmmm – could this be the source of the slang term stinko?)

The book also offers lots of helpful advice about Greek mannerisms.

They jerk their heads upward for no (which is pronounced OHI). They bow their heads once for yes. But here's the kicker: The Greek word for yes? Is nay. I sense trouble afoot already. A simple stroll through a colorful street market could easily become an exercise in garbled diplomacy.

Maybe I should stick to plain old American Southern English. After all, I am a stranger here.

As if they couldn't tell.

— May 1998

A Yacht in the Aegean

My favorite part of any Sunday newspaper is the travel section.

Yet, one can drive 20 miles around "town," and still not procure a Sunday edition of the Washington Post. I have actually snatched sections from the recycling trailer, or from fireplace baskets where I'm housesitting.

I just finished a travel section from a July edition of the Richmond paper. It did not take long; every article proclaimed the pleasure of cruises.

I detest cruises. I cannot imagine myself trapped on a towering, massive ship with thousands of tourists, even if I am one myself. I cannot imagine enduring the forced camaraderie, the assigned dining tables, the perky party hostess urging my participation in silly games.

I once went on a cruise. Once was enough.

I chose it carefully: Small boat, 30 passengers, different port each night.

My friend and I would sail around the islands of the Aegean Sea. I searched the Internet about Aegean sea life, but could find nothing. As I discovered once I was swimming in the deep blue Aegean, there is no sea life there.

Nothing was quite as expected aboard the Zeus III "yacht." I dubbed it "The Ugh Boat."

We were greeted not with a smiling welcome, but by a sullen, glaring Greek crew. Their command of English was akin to my command of their language.

We were advised about procedures, should it be necessary to abandon ship: "Jump into the water. We will pick you up later," the captain promised.

Our spirits sagged when shown our "superior first-class" cabin. The air conditioning consisted of a four-inch hole punched in the wall. The hole had a small vent that, when twisted by hand, wheezed a faint sigh of tepid air.

Our stateroom was nine-by-seven feet, most of it occupied by an oversized sink. The bathroom provided much hilarity during the week-long cruise. It measured 36-by-42 inches, and included a toilet situated atop a sort of stage. The 18-by-20 inch shower sat in a four-inch deep well. One glance and we knew shaving our legs would be unfeasible.

It was actually possible to take a shower while sitting on the toilet.

To shower, one stood in the well, lifted the sprayer attached to a rubber hose with a life of its own, and bravely turned the faucets. The hose roared to life, whipping around the tiny room, spraying the walls, the commode, the toilet paper and, at times, the bather. The hot water lasted about 90 seconds.

I have never bathed so infrequently as I did aboard the Zeus III.

Life aboard The Ugh Boat was akin to living aboard the Mir space station. The only difference is, we had gravity.

Here are some things I learned:

* To plan my day around escaping, as soon as we reached port, to a sidewalk café with a restroom.

* A swim in the sea can substitute for a shower.

* Not all Greek isles are picturesque; the island of Kea, for example, had all the charm and allure of Craigsville.

* Whenever you ask a Greek what something costs, he laughs maniacally and answers, "Nine million dollars!"

* When shopping in Tinos, those delightful little flasks with a picture of the Virgin Mary are for holy water, not scotch.

* Do not drink two glasses of wine at lunch and then shop for gold jewelry.

* It is unwise to rent a moped with the brand name "Apnea."

* Greek cemeteries are unique. Each tombstone features a glass "display case" of things important to that person in life. These included Coca Cola, ouzo, cigarettes and, oddly, a can of corn oil.

— August 2004

Something in Common, After All

I was enraptured by a photo on the cover of a catalog yesterday.
"Wherever it is, I want to go there!" I told Brownie as we walked up the driveway from the mailbox.

I figured it was probably Portofino, Italy, a place I've always wanted to go.

But then I looked closer, and realized I'd already been there. It was a photo of Mykonos, Greece. And immediately, I was transported across the Atlantic, and back into the dark blue Aegean Sea.

Sprinkled throughout the catalog were photos of various Greek places and people. All of them reminded me of something during my two weeks there.

A picture of the famous Greek cats reminded me of a night on the island of Paros, my very favorite of the isles I visited. I had escaped from my traveling companion – turns out, we didn't get along so well, after all – and was walking through the small winding streets alone. A cat leapt atop a fence and meowed at me. I stopped to pet and admire it. "Ooooh," I cooed. "You are a marvelous cat."

Then, I spotted an old Greek sea captain sort, sitting in a chair in the cat's yard. I had learned some Greek before I left, so I said good evening, and told him, as best I could, that his cat was pretty.

He revealed a near-toothless smile, and nodded. He held up a finger, as if to say, "Wait there." I did. He scrambled over to his garden and plucked something, and held it out as he walked toward me, still smiling. It was a giant sprig of fresh, fragrant basil. We petted the cat for few minutes, and then I said goodbye and continued on my way.

It was a small interaction between two disparate people who had something in common, after all. I felt quite happy.

Another page of the catalog had a photo of some aged Greek women, dressed head to toe in black.

This reminded me of the island of Naxos. I had again escaped on my own, and walked the streets, looking for adventure. I noticed a clothesline strung between two shops. On it hung about a dozen octopi. It was really weird, yet wonderful at the same time. Where else would one spy such a thing, except when traveling?

I walked on down to the tiny beach. I stepped into the water and looked down, discovering a rock of pure, white marble. Was it a broken piece of an ancient statue? I like to think so. Today, it sits in my bathroom, where I fondle and admire it often. Why buy souvenirs, when such things as rocks are right there?

After my swim, I sat on a towel on the sand for awhile. An old woman dressed head to toe in black came and sat on the rock beside me. She took off her heavy, sensible black shoes and rested her feet in the warm Aegean. We shared a smile. I plucked a pack of gum from my bag and offered her a piece. She smiled and nodded. Then, she rummaged about in the folds of her voluminous dark dress, and drew out two little cheese sandwiches. She offered me one, and I gladly accepted.

There, on the shores of the Aegean Sea, the old Greek woman and I ate our lunch, smiling and nodding, yet not speaking a word. It was a small interaction between two disparate people who had something in common, after all.

I might have stopped in a small Greek café and had some spanakopita and a glass of wine for lunch, believing myself to be blissfully alone. But then, I would have missed that wonderfully happy afternoon, without ever knowing it.

— February 2009

I Venture to Havana

There was much hullabaloo last week when former President Jimmy Carter trekked down to Cuba for a confab with Castro.

The TV news clips caused me to recall my own trips to Cuba, back in the late 1970s.

I was "working" as a writer in Key West. Out of sheer luck and happenstance, People magazine hired me to join the first Americans allowed into Cuba in 20 years.

The premise was wacky: Sonny McCoy, mayor of Key West, planned to slalom water-ski to Havana. Non-stop.

The ill-fated trip is a book in itself. Suffice it to say, Sonny didn't quite make it. The tow ropes rubbed his hands raw. He tried wearing two flowered oven mitts, but that left much dexterity to be desired. He climbed into the boat and rode most of the 90 nautical miles. Then, two miles out of Havana harbor, he slipped into his ski and waved like a conquering hero.

There's a whole funny story about us being surrounded by the Cuban navy, who hadn't been told to expect us. It includes amusing anecdotes about sailors pointing AK-47 machine guns in our faces, and Cuban divers searching our boats for bombs.

I had a ball.

My devil-may-care attitude served me well during the trip, or so I thought.

I merrily chatted with Cubans in the street. I sat beside Cuba's Minister of Tourism and peppered him with questions as we rode through the once-magnificent city. I laughed and joked and imagined myself quite charming.

I secretly taped everything on a tiny tape recorder Olympus had just introduced. I hid it in my pocket and felt deliciously spy-like throughout the trip.

Here's one thing I learned: When in a foreign country that isn't exactly cozy with the United States, pretend you're Canadian. The whole world loves Canadians.

One night, we went to Havana's famed Tropicana nightclub.

The floorshow was stunning. The daiquiris were tasty. The big band was excellent, if quirky: Instead of the standard "mufflers" on their trumpets, the players used construction hard hats.

Go figure. I learned that Cubans are some of the world's most resourceful folk.

Here's something else I learned: In Cuba, toilet paper is a hot commodity.

Upon entering the Tropicana restroom, I encountered a stern-faced matron in army fatigues. She handed each lady two – count 'em, two – squares of toilet paper.

It was like no other I'd seen, before or since. It was Russian-made, and a bright, garish shade of pink. It still had little splinters of wood in it.

Flushed with success, I returned home and soon learned that another group was planning the first Key West to Cuba yacht race in 20 years. I got a magazine assignment and signed up for my second jaunt to the Communist coconut isle.

We were to leave at 5:30 a.m. At midnight, my phone rang. It was the mayor.

"Margo, we've got a problem," he said. "The Cuban government has approved all 120 of us, except for you."

I had, indeed, made an impression.

"Before they let you in again, you've got to agree to three things," Sonny said. "First of all, they didn't like your sense of humor, so you cannot make any jokes while you're there. And you absolutely must not engage in political conversations with people in the street."

"What's the third thing?"

"Well," he said, "they're demanding you leave that little black tape recorder at home."

— May 2002

June: National Rural Laundry Month

Folks lucky enough to live in places without cookie-cutter subdivisions and homeowner's associations, without rules and regulations made by neighbors you don't really like, but must appease, know June's arrival means it's time to hang out the laundry.

To me, that's the best thing about spring and summer: Hauling a heavy basket loaded with wet laundry outside, brushing away the spider webs that sprung up overnight, and commencing to hang.

I actually have an "heirloom" clothespin holder – a cute little dress sewn together at the bottom. It's on a hanger, and filled with colored plastic pins. I had to hunt high and low to find those pins. Most commercial clothespins are wooden and flimsy; they get moldy when left on the line; they can give you a splinter, spoiling the overall laundry experience.

The colored plastic pins somehow fulfill me. I carefully match the pin color to the piece of laundry, or at least try to coordinate it. Sadly, the pins do not come in lavender, but they do come in pink.

I have a sort of fetish about hanging the laundry. All like items are hung together in groups, and color-coded within those groups. It's my own little OCD delight – a superbly organized line full of laundry, flapping in the breeze. Ahhhh.

I have several humorous memories of laundry from my childhood. First, there was the time my mother, a city girl just moved to the country, tried to shoo a skunk away from the clothesline with a dustmop. She thought it was an odd, yet rather pretty, cat. Then, there's the time my sister, having been ordered to hang her wet bathing suit on the line the minute we got home, did just that. We looked out the kitchen window and there she was, naked, way out yonder by the clothesline.

The story that commands the most laughter is Mom and The Bee. It points out one danger of hanging clothes outside in the fresh air. Mom and Daddy were going out that night, dressing in their bedroom. Suddenly, we heard high-pitched, feverish shrieking.

"Get it off me! Get it off me, David!" my mother hollered.

In the living room watching "Lost in Space," my sister and I were perplexed. What could be the matter?

A big bumblebee had nestled inside Mom's dress for a nap out on the line that afternoon. It had awakened grumpy and disoriented, and had furiously gone about doing what bees do: Stinging with a vengeance.

When I travel to foreign lands, I keep a sharp eye out for laundry. There's a lot more of it in Europe than, say, Richmond or McLean. Whenever I see it, I take a photo. While many travelers come home with pictures of statues and churches, I have lots of photos of foreign laundry. Some of them are framed.

One day on the Greek island of Santorini, I was strolling along and spotted a clothesline full of laundry. I was gratified to notice that it, too, was organized by color, type and size. I couldn't get a good shot from the sidewalk, so I looked around and, seeing no one, slipped just inside the front gate. As I stood there focusing my camera on the clothesline, I heard a motorbike.

Wouldn't you know, astride the scooter was the owner of the laundry. He threw open the gate, and cast me a castigating look. I tried to explain in rudimentary Greek – "Sorry" is one of the first words I try to learn in the local language – gesturing at his shirts and dishtowels and underwear flapping on the line, and then at my camera, smiling broadly all the while. Guidebooks for travelers rarely contain the phrase, "Sorry, but I love to take the pictures of your laundry."

He shook his head in disgust, and muttered something I did not understand. That was probably for the best. I did recognize the Greek words for "American" and "tourist."

I don't really know how I'd feel if I came home from a long day and discovered, say, a Ukrainian gentleman in my backyard, snapping pictures. Who knows? Perhaps this very minute, in a living room somewhere, there is displayed a framed photograph of my washcloths and underwear.

— June 2008

The Kinky Burglar

The only thing I dislike about winter is, by the time one gets home from work, it's dark. The only remedy to creeping and stumbling into a dark house is to leave the lights on all day. And my thrifty mother quashed that idea long ago.

Despite what she tried to instill in me, the true reason I don't leave the porch light on all day is, it will burn out sooner and it's a difficult, dirty job to change the bulb. It requires a screwdriver, never one of my favorite tools. In fact, it was just recently that I made the move from nail file to bona fide screwdriver in my little pink toolbox. For 40-some years, I made do quite nicely with a nail file/screwdriver, and a hairbrush/hammer. Don't even ask me the difference between pliers and a wrench.

Anyway, I came up my driveway the other night, cursing the anticipated darkness, to discover lights on inside the house. Strange.

Even stranger, the light that was burning was one I rarely use.

Then, I noticed a book where it had not been that morning.

"Someone's been in here," I thought.

This should have been no surprise, as I, like most other folks in the country, don't lock every door when I leave. I would, indeed, be hard-pressed to put my hands on my door key.

Upon closer inspection, I discovered an interloper had indeed been in my house. And left something quite nice on the kitchen counter.

That's the way things go in the country – if someone enters your house while you're gone, chances are they leave, rather than take, something.

I was astonished when I moved here from San Francisco to discover that some house doors actually had no keys.

When I requested the front-door key to my first house here, I was told, "Oh, that thing disappeared long ago." The big trouble was, the front door was permanently locked. No problem. There were three other doors. None of them had keys, either.

City folks cannot comprehend this facet of country living. A real estate agent I know had to delay a closing for two days while she found a locksmith and had a new key made for a testy couple from Northern Virginia.

The same was true in Key West. Only one of my houses actually had a key. And that one caused me a lot of embarrassment.

I was writing very late one night, clad in a silky little teddy and a bathrobe. I don't recollect why I suddenly needed to run outside for a minute, but I do recall that, as I did, the door slammed firmly shut behind me.

"Cripes. Now I'll have to climb in the kitchen window," I griped to myself.

I crept around to the side of the house. The window was high off the ground, but could be reached if I teetered atop the gas tank and stretched.

This was no job for a woman in a long, satin bathrobe. Before thinking things through, I took off the robe and tossed it into the open kitchen window. As I watched the robe fly through the air, it dawned on me this was a dumb thing to do. Now, I stood outside at 2 a.m. in a tiny teddy. What if I couldn't get through the window? Roam the streets, seeking assistance from a kindly stranger?

Gritting my teeth in determination, I managed to climb onto the gas tank. But the window was further away than I imagined. I reached for it, and then got stuck. The upper third of my body was inside, but my bottom was, well, sticking up in the air and going nowhere.

I hung there for awhile, kicking and thrusting, to no avail.

And then a spotlight hit me.

It was two Key West policemen. Driving by, they had spied what appeared to be a burglary in progress. Their guns were drawn as they approached, but they were laughing.

I managed to convince them that I was not a kinky burglar, but a damsel in distress. They put down their spotlight, holstered their weapons, and teamed up to push and heave me through the kitchen window. I tumbled to the floor. Then, they came around and rang the doorbell, asking to see my identification. They wanted proof I was not a kinky burglar, after all.

Then, they wanted coffee.

I thought they'd never leave.

— December 2006

I Am Handy!

I am beaming with the kind of pride only a handy homeowner can experience.

I am handy! Sort of.

I am the type who pays the housekeeper extra to teeter atop a ladder and change light bulbs in the ceiling. For most of my adult life, my home "tool box" consisted of the aforementioned hairbrush for a hammer, a nail file that doubled as a screwdriver, and some eyebrow tweezers that kind of worked as tiny pliers. These tools were quite adequate; there was a phalanx of handy, hunky men around, just hankering to do me a favor.

Those fellows have vanished, along with my waistline.

Several years ago, I showed my mother something I really, really wanted in a Christmas catalog. She gave me quite a quizzical look. But, she ordered it and wrapped it up in happy paper. It was a pink toolbox, filled with pink tools. Handy, and attractive, too!

Since then, I have periodically stalked around the house, looking for things that need fixing. Usually, I haul out the pink toolbox when I have pictures to hang. I go about this systematically, in an organized and focused fashion.

There are tools in the little pink box that I have never used, and never will. I have no idea what their intended use may be, other than, perhaps, a handy weapon. While they are pink, they look quite dangerous should they fall into the wrong hands. Those hands would likely be mine.

This week, necessity has enhanced my handiness.

It all started at the Clifton Forge Fall Foliage Festival. I was working a booth, and as soon as I arrived, folks started giving me things.

I hadn't eaten breakfast. Yet, the first woman I said hello to handed me a hot funnel cake. Another one gave me a cup of coffee. Ah, the breakfast of festival champions. Before long, friends I never knew I had were stopping by to say hello. One handed over a tasty apple turnover. Another managed to find, and present to me, a giant can of yams. We laughed and laughed; that is yet another story.

But, danger lurked in the happy crowd. I spotted him – he knows who he is – before he reached our table. He slunk slowly by, glaring at me. I pretended not to know him, but I know exactly who he is: Someone whose court trial I once covered; someone who wrote me threatening letters from prison. He is out now. His victim, though, died some time ago of complications from his injuries.

It is time to start locking my doors. Trouble is, I have no keys.

That meant new locking mechanisms, with new keys. That meant getting out the pink screwdriver and setting to work systematically, in a focused fashion. I surprised the heck out of myself by completing the task in less than an hour. I was handy!

This morning, I awoke to a very cold house. Just two days ago, I had the furnace cleaned. Today, it wasn't working. I went down to the cursed basement and examined the contraption. There was no reset button to be found.

I set to work systematically, in a focused fashion, and discovered that one panel of the furnace lifts off and, inside it, is the little red button. I carefully read the teeny tiny print, took a deep breath, and pressed the button. Presto! I am warm. I am handy!

— October 2008

In Praise of Pillows

Are you in love with your pillows?

I had thought I was quirky this way, until I began paying attention. I paid attention as I lugged my luggage to the front desk of various hotels. Even in the swankiest, there we were: The Pillow People.

I was surprised and delighted to learn recently that a friend is a Pillow Person just like I. We gigglingly confessed to one another that, until we were finished college, we had clung tightly to our childhood pillows.

I once ended a five-year romance when "someone" refused to turn around and head back to New Orleans to retrieve my pillows. After all, we were only 100 miles down the road.

There are a plethora of problems posed to Pillow People, especially when travelling. I have called the registration desks of various far-flung hotels, inquiring about the consistency and type and number of pillows in a typical room. The harried clerks seem disinclined to entertain my questions and concerns. They are not amused by my self-effacing anecdotes. Thus, I am forced to pack along my pillows.

And therein lies another problem. Pillows are bulky, unwieldy things. Wrestling them into a suitcase takes determination and dedication. Then, there's the problem of clothing, underwear and toiletries. Is there room?

I bought some plastic crush-sacks that reduce bulky things to the size of a fat wallet. They worked well a time or two; then, they ruined my precious feather pillows. Somehow, like the skin of an aging woman, they refused to spring back into perfection.

Hauling pillows along is no big deal if you're traveling by car. In fact, one can ensconce oneself in them and drive in great comfort – sort of an already-deployed air bag, but far more comfy. All that remains is to tote them into the hotel. This can raise eyebrows, as well as sneers, from bellhops and fellow guests. I have had travel companions turn aside and pretend they do not know me.

Traveling by train is somewhat more tricky, but still doable. It's the airlines that test the resolve of Pillow People. What with all the regulations of weight and number of bags, it is necessary to forego, say, extra pants and shoes and shirts, in order to fit in the pillows. You may not be well-dressed at your destination, but you will be well-rested.

I was forced to forego my pillows entirely when I flew to France. This was not good. Europeans have a different concept of pillows than we Americans. The so-called pillow (note singular usage) on my five-star hotel bed was forlorn. It was thin, and hard-bodied, much like the type of traveler to whom this hotel catered.

I had quite a bit of trouble communicating my desire for two – four, if you've got 'em – fluffy pillows to the hotel chambermaids. A small cluster of them surrounded me in the hall, uncomprehending looks on their faces. I grabbed the so-called pillow off my bed, cuddled it, and then pantomimed something larger and fluffier. They smiled, nodded, and brought me an extra blanket.

It has become necessary for me to buy four new pillows. Even two might do it, yet buying even one pillow is an arduous and difficult task. The perfect pillow cannot be ordered on-line. I live in a town where one cannot buy eyeshadow or underwear; need I mention I must make a 150-mile round trip to purchase a pillow?

The pillow section of department stores is puzzling. They are piled willy-nilly, not organized by firmness or type of filling. Worst of all, the pillows are covered in hard plastic. I am forced to fondle the packaged pillows, holding them against my head and trying to imagine if this is, indeed, my perfect mate. I guess the process would be akin to finding true love in a speed-dating bar.

My sweet sister, always on the alert for the ideal, and wonderfully-welcome gift, actually gave me four expensive new pillows last Christmas. I felt oh, so badly about it. They are plump but unyielding things, and they simply will not do. Naturally, they cannot be returned. They stand now, at the alert, on the guest room bed, ready to welcome the lone annual visitor.

Herein lies a lesson for careful gift-givers: Never try to please a Pillow Person. We are a quirky and quite picky lot. But to a man and/or woman, we are well-rested.

— August 2009

My Favorite Sentence

There was a magazine cover photo a few months back that I found particularly, well, titillating. The photograph was good-looking; full of come-hither promises; it stirred something within me.

It was a stack of books.

I have always loved and been excited by books. I collect them, as some collect knick-knacks or stamps or flamingos.

I'd rather buy books than clothes, as evidenced by the fact that I had a nice-sized closet renovated into a three-sided, floor-to-ceiling book nook. Still, I lack space for my ever-growing collection. Every now and then I promise myself, 'I must stop buying so many books.' I've got a penchant for hardbacks, you see; verging on $30 a pop, it's easy to drop a bundle in no time. Especially if Clive Cussler, Nelson DeMille, Carl Hiaasen, Lee Child and, oh, Philip Margolin issue simultaneous new releases.

That scenario actually happened this past winter. Thank heavens for public libraries.

Despite my penchant for television dramas, there are many nights when I'd much rather snuggle into my easy chair, light the fire, and read, read, read until my eyes can no longer focus on the words.

So, this year I decided to do something I've never had the time for before: Become a reading tutor at a local elementary school. What better way to share my love of books than to help some youngster learn to love them, too?

I'll admit, I had doubts. I am not a patient person, and patience seems to be a predominant prerequisite for a teacher. Heaven forbid I should heave a sigh, roll my eyes or, worse, snap at some struggling student.

I vowed to be easy-going (crossed my fingers on that one) and make the exercise fun for both of us.

My little fellow is in the second grade. He's a quiet, somber sort, or so he seemed during our first foray into the wonders of words. The going was slow and lacked luster. He kept checking his watch. He heaved a sigh. He rolled his eyes.

Then we came upon – in the same sentence, no less – the words "might" and "eight." Try explaining how to read and pronounce those words, and you'll know why most teachers have master's degrees. "There might be eight midgets in the aisle." Now there's a nightmare sentence for the novice tutor!

During our first session, I employed a technique where the student fills in every first letter he can think of to complete words such as _an, _at, _ad. Easy, eh? Well, not too.

During the _at exercise, he came up with "gnat." Uh oh. Another nightmare word to explain. To my surprise, he mastered it.

"I guarantee you're the only child in the second grade who can spell gnat!" I enthused at the end of our session.

He smiled for the first time. It was difficult to decide which of us felt more proud.

Finally, we progressed to the flash-card game. He seemed more excited about this aspect than about reading still more stories of hens and dogs and trains, so we focused on the words on the cards.

"You know," I told him. "We could make some fun sentences using just these cards."

He seemed interested. He forgot all about checking his watch.

I laid out all the cards on the table and told him to go for it. "Make up a really good sentence, using as many cards as you like," I said.

At first, his sentences made no sense; some began or ended with verbs, some had no verbs at all. I was not ready to explain the concept of a verb. He seemed to enjoy moving the gaily-colored cards around the table, so I let him have his fun.

"That's not a real sentence," I'd say. "I don't think I've ever heard anyone say, 'Had table boy keep sit place.' Have you?"

He'd laugh, and form another sort of sentence.

Then, his eyes lit up and his chubby little hands moved as swiftly as a magician's about the table.

"There!" he said, triumphantly.

"By golly, you've got it," I cried. "A real sentence!"

Together we read the sentence aloud.

"Man had fat tail; ate bad grass and ant cake."

We laughed until tears filled our eyes. In fact, I'm still laughing today.

"Man had fat tail; ate bad grass and ant cake."

It just might be my favorite sentence, ever.

— February 2002

Love a Teacher

When I think about teachers, I think about Miss Landes. Zona Landes was absolutely my favorite teacher. She taught English. It was she who first urged me to become a writer – "because of your imagination" – she would say, with a wry smile.

I must mention Mrs. Ruth Dalton, too. She, also, taught English, and also urged me to become a writer. Thank you, ladies, for putting ideas into my head!

I truly loved both of these women, and although Mrs. Dalton is gone to her heavenly reward now, I spot Miss Landes from time to time. This always causes me to break into a big smile and rush the poor dear. One great thing about getting older is, I can call her "Zona" without feeling guilty or disrespectful. She still employs that wry smile.

There was one teacher in elementary school with whom I most assuredly did not get along; the dislike was mutual between me and Miss Lucille Bonner.

Miss Bonner taught school and then was elementary principal for 50 years. She was a formidable woman with whom to contend, if you failed to measure up to her high standards. Miss Bonner detested that "imagination" of mine that Miss Landes later found remarkable.

One day, Miss Bonner and I got into a terrible row when she decided that, as a "recess activity," we could all go outside and pick up trash.

"I don't like getting dirty," I whined. "And besides, my father doesn't want me doing that."

"Well, I DO want you to do it."

This elicited a confrontation between Daddy, in his State Police uniform, and Miss Bonner, in her Shelton Stroller shirtwaist, shouting at each other behind closed doors. In the end, Miss Bonner "punished" me by making me sit in her office and read during recess. Ah, little did she know!

I never thought much about Miss Bonner until I began poking through files and boxes at the historical society. There on a shelf I found a treasure trove labeled "Lucille Bonner's scrapbooks."

I began leafing through them, and suddenly found myself thrust down Memory Lane. Regardless of how I once felt, I now regret that I did not know her better. After pawing through her keepsakes, I now understand how loveable Miss Bonner really was.

The photographs Miss Bonner pasted in her books are priceless.

"Warm Springs School, 1923" – one of her earliest years of teaching – shows Lucille and a host of other young lovelies, teachers all, draped across a shiny new Ford. Other photos give a glimpse into history: Picnic at Muddy Run, 1927; May Day at Millboro, 1926; Field Day at Valley High, 1928. What's more, Miss Bonner identified almost every person in every photo.

I know that some of you reading this recall Miss Bonner. Every person who went through the Bath school system for 50 years does.

Did you know that Miss Bonner saved every card signed by her students through the years? Did you know that, if you gave Miss Bonner a Christmas gift, your little tag with the childish printing is still in her scrapbook, with her notation of the gift written beside it? Perfume. Hankies. Stockings. It's all there, preserved for posterity.

If you got married between 1963 and 1978, your wedding announcement is pasted into Miss Bonner's book. It is not surprising she had a special affinity for wedding photos of her former students. She was a member of the Spinster's Club for more than 70 years; surely, she thought she'd die without ever becoming a bride herself.

But fate had a delightful surprise in store for Lucille Bonner. Along about 1985, an old sweetheart returned to sweep her off her feet. Fred Gleim was the only man Lucille Bonner ever loved. But he had headed north in the 1920s, while Lucille stayed in Warm Springs. Fred Gleim married, more than half a century passed, and then his wife died. He hied back to Warm Springs, scooped up Lucille and, at age 87, made her a blushing bride.

Ain't love grand?

— *August 2011*

Shattered Expectations

Friendships begin early and stay tight in rural locales.

I learned this sad lesson as a young child.

We moved from Northern Virginia to Bath County when I was in the middle of the second grade.

I went from a classroom of sixty students in an urban Catholic school, to a classroom of ten children in rural Virginia.

Talk about culture shock.

Mrs. Byrd was our teacher. She seemed overjoyed when, after testing, she learned I was reading at a ninth-grade level. She then made the mistake of sharing this with the other students in my class.

The other children were none too fond of me from the get-go. I guess, in retrospect, I was rather a prissy, over-achieving, know-it-all.

I'm happy to report that I'm now over my prissiness.

All the other children were natives to Bath County. Many of them were related. I recall my surprise at learning that most of them were cousins of some sort or other. I'm still trying to figure out what "twice removed" means.

The fact is, I had no friends.

I'd spent most of my childhood playing alone, and reading alone. Today, I adore being alone. But, as a second-grader, I was desperate for some friends to play with.

Well, my classmates were having none of it.

"Jan" and "Joan," the class Queen Bees, finally relented one fateful day.

"OK," they acquiesced, "we'll play with you tomorrow, if you bring your doll dishes to school."

Yippeeeee! I would have playmates.

The next morning, I trudged off to school toting my lovely little doll dishes in a special tiny suitcase. I was hap-hap-happy!

When the bell rang for recess, I could hardly contain myself. Jan and Joan grabbed the jump-rope and told me to follow them. As we headed to the farthest corner of our rural schoolyard, I noticed some of the boys were coming along, too. I thought it strange that boys would have an interest in playing with doll dishes.

When we reached the remote outpost, I got a nasty surprise.

The boys tied me to a tree with the jump-rope. Jan and Joan took my doll dishes and threw them in a deep ditch. Everybody laughed, except me.

We heard the end-of-recess bell ringing in the distance.

Everybody scampered back to class, except me.

There I was, alone in what I considered "the woods," tied to a tree with a jump-rope.

I was so mad, I began screaming at the top of my lungs.

Finally, thank heavens, Mrs. Byrd noticed my absence and came looking for me.

She untied me. Together, we went to take a look in the deep ditch. My lovely doll dishes were broken to bits. The little suitcase was unhinged, and ruined. No need for it now, anyway, I sighed.

We marched back to the school, where Mrs. Byrd deposited me in the office while she called my mother. Mom, in turn, managed to reach my father at work.

Soon, Daddy arrived. He concentrated while Mrs. Byrd related the sad tale. I watched his lips whiten, and then turn a little green around the edges. This was a sign Daddy was very mad. This was never a good sign, except for that day.

Did I mention Daddy was a Virginia State Trooper?

Did I mention he was in uniform, having received the call while on patrol?

Daddy took me by the hand, and together, we marched into the classroom.

Daddy addressed the class, advising them of the sorts of laws that had been broken. He could, if he were of a mind, arrest all of them, he noted.

(This of course was not true, but then, what do second-graders know?)

While all of this made me feel a little better, it did nothing to improve my opportunities to make lasting friendships among those other nine children.

Some of them, I meet in passing today – at the post office, the grocery store, some community event. We smile and chat about the weather, inquire after each other's health and family. Then, we move on as if a kidnapping, robbery and assault never happened.

When you live in the country, you've got to learn to forgive and forget.

— April 2007

Somebody 'Laves' Me

This time of year, parents are packing their kids off to camp.

The usual joke about this is that the parents are secretly delighted to be ridding themselves of the little darlings for a couple weeks. But I have a feeling that the real joke is on them: The kids are more than delighted to be leaving home.

I was desperate to go to 4-H camp when I was a kid. It was "only $40 a week," I kept telling my parents. But apparently, $80 was a lot of money at the time. Anyway, I was left at home, reading alone all summer, while the other kids cavorted at camp.

Finally, the summer came when my parents acquiesced. The joke was probably on me: They wanted me out of the house as much as I wanted to be set free. So, off to Holiday Lake I went.

Holiday Lake. Why, the very words conjure up fabulous days and nights of wonder. They do not cause one to conjure up sleeping on cots in a musty cabin with 10 other girls. And countless spiders.

Here are my memories of that summer at camp: First, nearly drowning when another kid kicked my head while I was swimming underwater. A girl named Brenda Arehart, who'd been assigned my "buddy" even though I knew I didn't need one, pulled me out of water. I regained consciousness sprawled on the floating dock, a handsome older man of 16 giving me artificial respiration. I got tingly with excitement; the fact I was going to live was secondary.

I do recall my favorite meal at camp: The night the oven broke, and the cook served cake batter for dessert. I've always liked the batter better than the cake.

Most of all, I recall falling in love. The promise of romance is the rosiest thing any girl can conjure up at 13.

It happened on the dance floor, as all great romances should. Either Elvis or the Righteous Brothers provided the mood music; either will do, at 13.

His name was Wayne Snead. He was very tall, and dark, and certainly as handsome as Elvis. (At that age, Elvis was the paramount standard to which I held all men).

To make the evening even more special, my best friend Linda Hite was falling in love on that very dance floor, too. His name was Nicky Scaboo. In the ensuing years, I've yet to meet anyone else with a name that conjures up more fun: Nicky Scaboo.

At the boys' suggestion, Nicky and Linda and Wayne and I slipped away from the dance floor for a walk in the moonlight. And it was there, somewhere under the whispering pines and a full moon at 4-H camp, that I got my first kiss.

Wayne and I were inseparable the rest of that week. I was elated: Not only was I at some exotic locale, away from home, I had also acquired my first boyfriend!

We sat close together on the bus back home, and Wayne kissed me 14 times. At that age, a girl counts those types of things.

After we returned, Wayne sent me a note. Starry-eyed, I showed it to my father. At that age, a girl does those types of things. The note said this: "I lave you. Wayne."

My father read it with a stony face.

"It says here he laves you," he noted. "Do you know what that means?"

"Oh yes!" I cried. "He loves me!"

"No. He 'laves' you. That means he wishes you would wash," Daddy said, bursting into laughter.

Fathers really know how to quash a romance.

So, if you're packing your daughters off to camp this summer, be advised: They could come close to drowning, be bitten by spiders, consume dangerously undercooked food, and be kissing strange boys until their lips turn purple.

On the other hand, they'll be out of the house for two weeks.

— July 2003

An Unhappy Camper

Well, it's almost vacation time.

Are you desperate to get out of town? Are you longing for the bright lights of a big city? Or, would you rather trek into the woods, build a campfire, and commune with nature? Can you guess which option I'd choose?

I have never been a happy camper. There are just too many icky, tricky things involved. Back when I was wildly in love, I allowed myself to be talked into a camping trip. I focused on the aspects that were positively romantic, rather than the reality.

Our trip began nicely enough. We borrowed a tent, and everything that goes inside one. I provided a gaily-colored set of plastic picnic dishes and utensils. I packed all kinds of things I could imagine us sharing for breakfast, lunch and dinner. And, I smartly decided to bring along a bottle of scotch. Who knew that scotch would be the smartest thing I could have packed?

We traipsed into the forest and set up a little weekend love nest, far from the madding crowds. (I can never fathom why people go into the woods to camp, and then surround themselves with hordes of other campers. Seems about as much fun to me as spending a few days in a hurricane evacuation shelter.)

We built a cozy little campfire and frolicked in a stream. My companion, a self-proclaimed expert, began to impart all sorts of camping tips.

"Several times a day, we have to check each other for ticks," he said.

"Huh?" This idea seemed not even remotely romantic.

"This is how," he said, as he began running his fingers through my hair. I was reminded of monkeys in the jungle.

"Aha!" he cried. "There's one!"

I fervently hoped that this was a joke of some sort, and inquired about that very thing.

It was no joke. We had been in the woods for less than hour, and somehow a tick had burrowed its horrid way into my head.

I became quite upset, and started to weep a little. I began to blabber about clean sheets and room service.

"Do you have any tweezers?" he wondered.

Tweezers were not among the many, many things I had packed. Even

I knew that intense personal grooming tasks can be abandoned during a weekend in the woods.

"Did you happen to bring a lighter?" my companion inquired.

Indeed I had, but I was not about to hand it over to someone with his hands in my hair.

"I'll have to think about what to do," he said, starting to pace.

I knew exactly what to do: Panic. I had seen ticks before. While dog sitting, I discovered huge things clinging to a dog's fur. I placed a concerned call to the owners.

"Oh, those are just ticks," they said, unfazed. "Pull them off, and drop them in that jug of gasoline out in the woodshed."

The idea was utterly abhorrent. Nonetheless, we tramped out to the woodshed and performed the ghastly duty. To this day, even thinking about it turns my stomach. I furtively surveyed our campsite. We had no gasoline. This made me almost happy. Gasoline, lighters, hair: Three words no woman wants to hear used in the same sentence.

"We've got to get that little sucker out of there," my companion mused.

By this time, my choices were two: Freak out completely and run screaming from the woods, never to return; or, try to calm down and brace myself for the ordeal ahead.

"Bring me the scotch!" I cried.

"Hey," he said, "that's not a bad idea."

He rummaged through the supplies and came trotting back over, bottle in hand.

"Surely you don't expect me to slug it out of the bottle," I whined. "Bring me a cup."

"Watch this," he said. He unscrewed the cap and poured a few drops into it. "Bend down," he demanded.

I had no idea what might be coming, but I did as directed. He then poured the scotch onto the tick in my head.

"It's backing out!" he yelled.

Sure enough, the little bloodsucker had quickly exited my scalp. He enjoyed a happy death, I presume, drowning in a capful of premium-brand liquor.

It took far less time to "break camp" then it did to set things up. I walked briskly, but did not run, from the woods. I did not scream. I will never return.

— April 2009

I Love to Snovel Show!

Spring is on the horizon.
That means we'll probably have a foot of snow before Easter.
Snow makes me think of a one-time driveway. Paved, and very, very steep. Often, I couldn't get the car all the way up, and had to leave it where it sat, perilously close to the busy highway.
One memorable day, the little car gave me all it had, and then gave up on the icy pavement. I had just finished a long trip, and was anxious to use my facilities. I hustled up to the house, as quickly as one can on foot, in ice and snow.
In less than 90 seconds, the phone rang.
"Margo, your car has rolled across the highway and crashed into my mother-in-law's fence," a neighbor reported. "A big log truck almost creamed it when it crossed his path."
I'd about had it with that cursed driveway.
As it happens, one of my favorite winter activities is shoveling snow. That paved driveway, probably just 1/8 of a mile long, provided lots of exciting exercise. I'd start at the top and, by the time I'd shoveled my way to the bottom, I swear I'd lost five pounds.
My face was beet red. My hair was soaked, and sticking to my head. I'd stand there at the bottom, holding the shovel aloft in a victory gesture. People in cars passing on the highway would gape at me in alarm. Surely, I resembled a heart attack just about to happen. Every now and then, a passenger would holler out the window, "Are you okay?"
"I love to snovel show!" I'd shout, clearly almost out of my mind with the heady exertion.
One winter morning, things took a bad turn. Lots of snow had been predicted. I awoke excited, and then plunged into dejection when I looked out the window and saw just an inch or so of white.
I was wearing a green sweatsuit. I put on my red jacket, and headed down the driveway to retrieve the morning newspaper from the box.
About half-way down, I discovered that the driveway was a sheet of black ice.
I realized this as I was flying backward up in the air, and then crashing down to the asphalt, my full weight cracking on the top of my head.
"Good God, that hurts," I said to myself. My next thought was, "This is very, very bad."

I tried to get up and could not. I managed to crawl a few feet over to the snow, and then collapsed into it, face first. I turned my head and looked up at my house.

"I know that's my house," I thought, "but I can't remember what my kitchen looks like."

I lay like that for awhile. It was very cold. My head was on a pillow of soft snow. I remember convincing myself that this was actually quite nice. Peaceful, even.

"I'll just take a little nap," I thought. "Then, I can get up and walk back to the house."

The next thing I remember, that neighbor was shouting at me.

"Margo, you've fallen and you can't get up," he said, not appearing to be joking. He threw a blanket over me. "I've called the rescue squad."

"Okay," I smiled. "I'm just taking a nap."

The neighbor's mother-in-law was one who sat by her window much of the day, keeping a watchful eye on the goings-on. For awhile that morning, she had watched an odd lump across the road. She'd wondered, "What is that in Margo's driveway?"

She'd deduced that the red and green blob must be a discarded Christmas tree. It was, after all, January 6. Finally, though, she realized that the lump was Margo.

Soon the rescue squad arrived with six members and a gurney. They were very solicitous and kind. I was grateful to see them, but quite disoriented. I was also worried. I just knew that, once they loaded me onto that gurney and picked it up, they would be able to guess my weight.

If they did guess, they were too polite to mention it.

— February 2007

The Pokey-dokes

I call them pokey-dokes. I call them lollygaggers. I can't reveal what I call them when I'm really pressed for time.

One bane of rural living is our two-lane roads. While I look upon this as a blessing whenever I travel in six or eight lanes of interstate traffic, I mutter with frustration about it every workday.

Under ideal conditions, it takes 12 minutes to drive from home to the historical society. But rarely are conditions ideal. Invariably, one must contend with pokey-dokes and lollygaggers.

There are just two passing zones between Healing and Warm Springs. Surely I'm not the only one who looks oh-so-forward to reaching them, in order to zip around whatever's impeding my progress. I often chuckle to myself as I pass, because to do so does not even require reaching the speed limit. When you can pass another vehicle and still not exceed 48 miles an hour, chances are you've encountered a pokey-doke.

Pokey-dokes fall into several categories.

"The Coot in a Cockeyed Cap." The crusty old coot, sporting the requisite cockeyed cap, can be found behind the wheel of a wheezing pickup truck that spews oil fumes. The truck often bears "farm use" tags. This always leads me to wonder, why is he not back on the farm? The Coot constantly swivels his head to either side. I'm convinced he's looking for deer he can come shoot later. The Coot's companion is a dog of indeterminate pedigree. The hound hangs on for dear life in the bed of the truck, which is loaded with trash and bald tires.

"The Wispy White-haired Dear." The Dear is usually driving her late husband's 1987 Oldsmobile. Her wispy white halo frames the steering wheel, over which she can barely see. Be assured, the Dear is going only one of three places: church, the supermarket, or the beauty parlor. To add to the excitement, the Dear likes to drive with her left-turn signal blinking at all times.

"The Dart-n-Dawdler." That darned Dart-n-Dawdler has a habit that annoys me to no end: He darts into traffic right in front of my car, in one hell of a hurry. Once in the stream of traffic, however, he dawdles and dallies. The irony of this is, if you check your rear-view mirror, you will discover miles of open highway behind you; had the Dart-n-Dawdler waited just five seconds, he'd have had the road all to himself.

"The Swerving Line Hog." The Hog likes to hug the center line, swerving over it from time to time. The Hog is usually driving some monster vehicle, wide and tall; it is impossible to see over or around him to ascertain whether you might pass, should one of the two opportunities present itself.

The point of passing is most often moot. The "Murphy's Law" of driving is this: When the anticipated passing lane looms ahead, so will an oncoming vehicle. It does not matter that not a single vehicle has been heading in the opposite direction throughout your trip; when your opportunity to pass a pokey-doke arrives, it will be thwarted without fail.

And then, there are the Lollygaggers. The lollygaggers, God bless 'em, are tourists on vacation. They're not just from out of town, they're probably from out of state. They're used to driving on the beltway, or in the suburbs. They're marveling at the wonders around them, including the two-lane blacktop we traverse everyday. They're looking for restaurants, for motels with vacancies, for gas stations. They're awed by the grand hotel, the cows in the meadow, the groundhog on the side of the road.

The point is, they're not paying attention to driving. The point is, they're impeding the progress of locals who must get to work, and go about their everyday lives. Tourists, please know we appreciate your visit; now, please get on down the road!

Funny thing, but my frustration with tourists flies out the window the very minute I become one myself. Then, it is I who am looking for a restaurant, or a museum entrance, or a street address. Then, it is I who am lollygagging along, marveling at the scenic views.

And, invariably, some impatient shlub who's late for work zips past, shaking his head and muttering in his rearview mirror.

— May 2004

The Rural Wave

Yesterday, I was catching up with a friend from Northern California, who also owns a place in Warm Springs. He'd just made the drive across the country, and he was still shaking his head in awe about something.

It's endemic.

It's uniquely ours.

It's the Rural Wave.

You won't find it in Fairfax, or Norfolk, or the Napa Valley.

But, drive just a few miles on a country road, and you'll encounter it at nearly every turn.

A pickup will pass and, as it does, the driver will wave. At you. A stranger.

Visitors are perplexed, if not amused. Especially those from urban areas where, if a stranger in a passing car lifts a finger, it's usually the middle digit.

Around these parts, folks have perfected the one-finger wave. In no way does it impede their driving. The index finger is simply lifted, briefly, and then returns to the steering wheel. There is seldom a nod, and certainly not something so flamboyant as a smile.

Chances are, an SUV full of Maryland tourists are led to think, "What did he mean by that?"

But after the fourth or fifth wave from the fourth or fifth vehicle, they get it: The natives are friendly!

There are all sorts of rural waves. The most prevalent is the "one finger salute." The greeting can be doubled – two fingers off the wheel – a throwback to the old "peace" sign. On odd occasions, a driver will lift each index finger. One gesture you will never see in rural locales is that city hipster thing where the thumb and little finger are raised in a Randy Jackson way. And never, ever, will a rural local actually "wave," with all fingers up and moving. That one's personal, reserved for immediate family.

There are all sorts of interesting social aspects here. First, most wavers are men. Women are wont to wave, lest we be thought too friendly. Many of the waving men are driving pickup trucks. The older and slower the truck, the more apt a driver will be to wave. A passing Mercedes, Lexus, or Jaguar driver almost never bestows a wave.

Men wearing ties just don't have time to wave. They are busy thinking about business.

Ditto for cell phone users. Frankly, we'd rather a driver yakking on a cell phone not lift yet another finger from the wheel.

My California friend was amazed that, as he drove some 3,000 miles to get here – taking the scenic route through Montana – not one driver waved until he reached Route 39 between Millboro and Warm Springs.

"After that," he noted, "I think nine drivers out of 10 waved at us."

This fellow drives throughout the United States, Mexico, and Canada. "The only time I ever recall being waved at, other than here," he says, "was someplace out in God's Lost Texas."

All things considered, I'd rather be waving in beautiful Bath County.

I strive to wave, unless I'm having a particularly grumpy day. Once, however, I was gripping the wheel to avoid a squirrel, and I inadvertently raised my middle finger from the wheel. I can't seem to forget it; I guess the person to whom I sent the gesture is still wondering, too.

Why do we rural folks wave?

I think it's because we live and work and play in a small town. We know almost everyone, whether we like them or not. And even if we don't "cotton to" someone, we will, by rural decree, have to have intercourse with them sooner or later.

So, we wave at every car; this is no place to be discerning. Our friends are happy. Our detractors are distracted. Our tourists are confused, but soon enough, they're smiling.

Is it any wonder they're still smiling when they get to their hotel? Is it any wonder they want to come back again? Is it any wonder so many decide to move here and make this place their own?

— July 2007

Dancing the Dance

When I lived in San Francisco, I learned to, as they say, "Walk the walk and talk the talk." No mistaking me for a country girl, no sirree.

But now I'm a country girl again. And when you live in the country, you'd better learn to "dance the dance."

Thus it was that I found myself in a country line-dancing class. I'm not too familiar with country music, so I started out with a distinct disadvantage: I didn't know my Achy-Breaky Heart from my Boot Scoot Boogie. When "all my rowdy friends" come over, we sip chardonnay and watch "Masterpiece Theater."

There aren't a lot of cultural opportunities around these here parts, so when "DJ Willy" offered a country line-dancing class, I jumped at the chance to have some fun and learn something new.

First, as always, there was the perplexing problem of what to wear. I own no cowgirl boots. I have one pair of jeans. I don't have a Western shirt with pearl buttons, and in place of a string tie I settled for a jaunty pink bandana. I rummaged around in my closet and pulled on an old pair of jodhpur boots. "These will have to do," I shrugged.

Fully attired, I looked like one of the Village People on an estrogen high.

Those of us gathered in the elementary school cafeteria represented a broad cross-section of folks ranging in age from five to 73.

The first thing we learned was the Electric Slide. It's not exactly a "country" dance, but I've found that wherever dancers gather, someone soon enough breaks into the Electric Slide and everyone joins in. Everyone, that is, but me. I was determined to learn the Electric Slide, even if it is 15 years out of date.

We did not learn the Macarena. That's a shame, because I remember it. I could easily qualify as the Diva of Obscure Dances; I also remember the Bristol Stomp, the Mashed Potato and the Bump. We did not do those dances, either.

Instead, we learned the Honky-Tonk Stomp, the Watermelon Crawl and, sure enough, the Boot Scoot Boogie. We also learned something called the Tush Push. It was rather tricky, especially if you've got a lot of tush to push. There's shuffling and hopping and clapping to be done, all of it quickly and precisely.

"It's simple, really," Willy said, urging us onward. You shuffle, you hop, you clap."

"Well," I called out, "I've got the clap."

The double entendre hit all of us about the same time. It's easier to dance if you're laughing. But it's hard to laugh if you're red-faced and your heart is racing.

"Thank God we've got a nurse in our midst," someone panted.

"Yeah, well, I'm too out of breath to help," the nurse was quick to retort.

Most of the adult dancers were put to shame by a gaggle of giggling seventh-grade girls who effortlessly romped through the moves. And there were a few grown-up "ringers" – folks who danced as if they'd been scooting boots for decades. The rest of us concentrated on our heel-toe-stomp-stomps and our one-two-three-kicks, huffing and puffing and having a grand old time.

"Remember to smile!" Willy encouraged us. Somehow, we did. We even managed to holler "Yeeee, haaaaa!" now and then.

At the end of one class, a young, lithe woman came up to me.

"You are hot!" she exclaimed.

I pranced around rather proudly until I caught a glimpse in the mirror. My hair was plastered to my head; my crimson face glowed with sweat. She'd meant it literally.

— January 2006

On the Rivah

I'm lucky I didn't break my arm.

I'm sort of lucky only three women saw me half-naked, changing clothes behind my car.

I'm probably lucky that kayaking season is over.

This summer, a gaggle of giggling women enjoyed Tuesday Flotillas down the Jackson River. We'd gather at 5 o'clock at the comfy family camp of our hostess. A half-dozen or more of us would load kayaks into her old farm pickup, and then we'd drive a few miles up the Jackson.

There, we'd drink wine while unloading the kayaks, then clamber inside them, and be pushed off the shore and into the swift water.

The Jackson appears quite placid, until it grabs hold of your kayak and takes you where you may as well want to go.

I am not sporty. But, I spent half my life as a "waterbaby" of one sort or another, so I'm always eager when a water opportunity arises.

We all had lifejackets. We used them as cushions against the hard plastic seats. Comfort is paramount when women reach a certain age.

The more adventurous and experienced sipped pinot grigio as they floated and swirled. I grabbed hold of my oars (or whatever) and gritted my teeth, prepared to battle the river.

I suppose our whoops and guffaws and squeals disturbed the peaceful surrounds. I did see a fisherman who was none too pleased when a fleet of fun-time floozies floated past.

The last August Tuesday was our final flotilla of the season. It might have been my last altogether.

I was confident, attacking the Jackson's rocks and eddies. "I'm ready for you!" I shouted.

As I drifted, I thought I might buy my own kayak. "This is fun and easy; I could do it alone!"

I ditched that idea when a strong current swept me at rapid speed toward a large tree limb, hanging at face height. It was too low to the water for me to duck and cover. I flung up my right arm to block it. Big thorny brambles surrounding the foot-thick limb grabbed my flesh and dug deep. My paddle, raised to ward off the tree, became entangled in the branches.

I was stopped dead in a rush of swift water.

The others paddled past me, hopeless to help.

"Are you OK?" each hollered as they sped away.

"I'm stuck!"

"Good luck!" they could only cry.

Our capable hostess beached her boat and forged on foot through the rapids. Once untangled, I, too, was swept away.

"Good luck!" I could only cry.

Safely back at camp, our group of 12 was joined by a dozen more ladies. There was just one man, and he was there to cook. Life is good!

Our chef said his goodbyes as we sat down to dinner.

And then a poor dumb bat flew inside.

Words cannot convey the chaos and hubbub, the shrieks and screams, as 24 women attempted to duck the bat as he buzzed the buffet line. Someone turned off all the lights, but that caused us to bump into each other, spilling barbecue and lobster salad.

Finally a Texas girl, who's not scared of much, grabbed a fishing net on a long rod and, like a lacrosse champ, snagged the bat and flung it out the door.

I'm happy to report not a single wine glass was broken.

I will miss everything about our Summer Tuesday Flotillas, except the bats and bugs. But I've decided against buying my own kayak anytime soon.

— October 2006

The Surprise Wedding

I love to read wedding accounts in city newspapers.

The Richmond paper recently announced a wedding in Ben Lomond, California. This lovely, rural locale is the heartland of all things counter-cultural.

The bride's photo looked quite normal, until one noticed feathery angel wings affixed to the back of her gown. Her brother, identified as a "Wizard" rather than a Reverend, "officiated at the double-tattoo ceremony."

If I must witness tattooing, please serve my champagne prior to the ceremony.

The bride was "escorted by dancing woodland fairies and other forest beings."

At most weddings, the groom is a colorless yet necessary character. Not so here. This California son was "resplendent in white formal attire and derby, embellished with kaleidoscopic braid and feathers." He was followed by "frolicking elves."

Something tells me this couple did not register a china pattern.

The ceremony concluded "with a burning of the groom's interactive sculpture, The Swirling Cosmic Mystery."

Probably a good idea.

My favorite account is the couple who tied the knot on an Amtrak train. The bride used duct tape and safety pins to decorate the wedding coach. I admire a resourceful woman.

The groom's "hair was freshly permed." I admire a man who's unashamed to reveal his personal beauty regimen.

After the wedding, the couple returned home to "finish sheet-rocking the upstairs hallway." I admire practicality.

Like many modern couples, this one had honeymooned the summer before the wedding. I admire a couple who plans ahead.

In a move that showed sound thinking, children were corralled into a roped off "entertainment zone," so adults could "enjoy the festivities freely."

And the first dance was far from traditional. To the strains of "We Are Family," more than 90 guests joined the couple in a "festive conga line." Is it any wonder the reception "lasted into the wee hours"?

Reading further, we learn how the bride's training helped her pull off the gala event: She's a specialist in controversy management and disaster planning.

Would that I had her assistance with my own wedding.

True to our fly-by-night natures, one morning we decided to get married. Since the planning of anything was always my job, Tom decided he'd work that day, while I raced to Hot Springs and gathered the necessities.

I hustled around the house, grabbing a dress and a pair of ivory, kid-leather French shoes. With fabulous shoes, a girl can do anything. I broke the news to Mom by calling to ask, "Do you have anything old and blue that I can borrow?"

"I certainly hope so," she sighed.

I hied back to Lexington with my "trousseau in a shoebox." Tom was still working, so I laid out what among his jumble of clothes might pass for wedding attire. It was July, so I chose white shorts, a new blue shirt, and then rummaged around for some clean socks.

I should mention that Tom, a very dear, kind-hearted fellow, is the biggest slob I've ever had the pleasure to know. He never picks up or puts away anything; it's all just compost for the big tangle. He blames it on growing up in the Pentagon Athletic Club. But that's another story.

We planned to meet the Justice of the Peace at 4:30. By 4:13, Tom was not yet back from work. By 4:25, he had dashed in, jumped in the shower, and, dripping wet, climbed into his wedding clothes.

We sped downtown. That's when I discovered he wasn't quite sure where the Justice's office was. And – oops, almost forgot – there was still the license to procure. We asked the harried court clerk where we might find the Justice, only to learn that there is no such person. We hurried across the street to the office of an attorney who performs marriages.

His secretary would "have to see if he is in," she said. She directed us to the waiting room. That's when Tom noticed that the zipper on his shorts was broken. The little teeth were off track. He couldn't close the gaping hole. I remembered a trick my mother taught me: If you pull the zipper all the way up and fold it over – voila! – it would work.

"I'll fix it!" I cried.

I fell to my knees and closely inspected the zipper. I grabbed it and attempted the trick. The secretary gaped at us, aghast. We overheard her speak urgently into the phone.

"You'd better hurry," she told the attorney. "They're quite anxious."

— *August 2004*

I Learn New Tricks

Boy, have I got a lot to learn.
They say you can't teach an old dog new tricks.
Well, my new dog needs to learn a few old tricks.

I was sad to learn that Brownie, my new little dog, does not know what a dog is supposed to do with a ball. Hint: chase it, bring it back to me, and then we'll do it all again.

Brownie watches the ball roll by; then, she looks at me as if I'm daft.

If a dog could say, "So what?" that's what I'd hear from Brownie about her new green ball.

In fact, Brownie doesn't know anything about anything to do with toys.

Here was another big surprise: I was excited to make a deposit at the bank's drive-through the other day, because I finally had a dog in the seat beside me.

Every dog I know, knows that driving past the bank window means one thing: Biscuits! I once cared for a dog, Ozzie, who actually honked the horn, he was so anxious to get his bank biscuit.

Not Brownie. She sits there quietly on her little blanket. She looks at the biscuit, sniffs it, and goes back to sleep.

Should I need a spare doggie biscuit, I know just where to find one: it's been sitting on my passenger seat for five days now.

I figured that, sooner or later, she'd figure it out.
But no.
Here's something I've had to learn: how to housebreak a grown dog.

I never thought to ask, before I adopted her, if Brownie was housebroken.

I naturally assumed that a four-year-old dog knows that business gets done outside.

Imagine my dismay to learn otherwise.

I've had Brownie almost two weeks now, and we've learned the housebreaking thing together. I'd say she's 90 percent of the way there. It's that remaining 10 percent that can vex one.

I'll say this: Never have I spent so much time outside.

I'm outside at 6 a.m. in my pajamas, watching a dog's hind end.

I'm outside at 8 a.m., and again at 10. I'm outside at noon, watching a dog's hind end. Finally, when my day ends about midnight, I'm standing outside in the dark, in my pajamas, watching a dog's hind end.

It's actually quite nice out there, when I can make myself focus on nature, rather than nature's call.

Here's something else I had to learn: how to coax, and finally push, a little dog into a big crate. I've also learned to endure the pitiful wailing as I leave the house, and the pitiful wailing that greets me upon my return.

I hope my neighbors aren't disturbed by the pitiful wailing. But I am.

I've learned that the best, easiest, most fun thing to do is to just bring Brownie along on my travels.

Brownie is now a welcome guest at the nursing home and at friends' houses. She's the most social dog I've ever known. Sunday, she served as the greeter at the elementary school all afternoon, as artists brought in their work for the Bath County Art Show.

Just about everyone gushed and cooed at Brownie, even those who nearly tripped over her short little doggie self.

I've learned that almost everyone is friendlier if you've got a little dog at your side. This is a good thing, wouldn't you agree? We could all stand to see a few more happy faces.

My face is a lot happier now that I have a happy little dog. I like it when I can start the day by laughing out loud. And end the day standing out under the stars, in my pajamas, watching a dog's hind end.

— July 2006

Brownie the Party Dog endured with good grace the placing of a party hat on her furry head.

The Party Dog

Welcome to the occasional adventures of Brownie the Party Dog.

Brownie was specifically invited to two parties last weekend. She is quite the popular little dog; a social animal, if you will. She is well-behaved, doesn't drink too much, doesn't laugh too loudly, or unintentionally insult anyone. She is the guest who is happy to come, and happy to leave. She does not overstay her welcome.

The first gathering was an intimate affair, just three humans and Brownie the Party Dog. Our host and hostess were happy to welcome Brownie; they even had a pretty little water dish for her. Actually, it was a teacup, but Brownie didn't mind. Her eye, you see, was on the snacks.

A small, low table had been set on the porch with comfy chairs and an expansive view of the Warm Springs Valley. We were high on a hill, in a yard I was assured was "completely fenced." The table was laden with special cheeses, some yummy dips, and lots of fancy crackers. Brownie loves crackers. And cheese.

She was certain the spread had been laid out especially for her. It was, after all, at her eye level. Oh, a tableful of tasty things. Brownie the Party Dog was all a-wag, a big smile on her face.

I know how these things go – once Brownie gets a small snack from the table, the feast has begun. I advised our hosts not to give the little dog a taste of anything until we were finished consuming as many snacks as we might wish.

We spoke nicely to Brownie, but did not bestow any snacks. She seemed dejected, and wandered into the wonderful yard. Brownie stays close to "home," wherever that may be, as a general rule. Except when she does not.

We got involved in our conversations, and lost sight of Brownie. No matter; the yard was completely fenced. Except, I suddenly remembered, for the stone posts at the end of the half-mile driveway. Which sits across busy Route 220 from the high school.

Brownie did not answer my calls. I went looking. She could not be found. I was frantic.

At the high school, the band was playing. Children were shouting and laughing. There were people – far more than we three who were ignoring her – so Brownie had chosen, I feared, a far more lively venue. The little dog had marched down the long driveway, crossed the busy road, and joined the bigger party. Luckily, someone read her little pink dog tag. And someone else recognized her. She was delivered to my arms in a rather guilty state.

Saturday night, we attended a large party in a large yard. Eighteen children were in attendance. They welcomed Brownie the Party Dog. She was in her glory. Then, dinner was served.

Brownie went into a party food frenzy. She stalked a toddler wobbling across the yard, carrying a plate laden with smoky little wieners. Snatch! The wieners were gone. So were the peaches, which were quickly spit onto the grass. Wagging her entire body, smiling large, Brownie continued on her quest, snarfing chips and pasta salad and bits of ham. Guests pretended not to mind.

Then, I caught sight of her among the crowd of 60 or so. Someone had placed an iced tea cup on the grass beside their chair. Thirsty after all the purloined party food, Brownie was lapping up the tea.

The Party Dog attempted to make amends for her indiscretions by allowing herself to be placed in a red wagon and pulled around the yard in a sort of Party Parade, surrounded by frolicking, gleeful children. I know that everyone under 10, including Brownie the Party Dog, had a marvelous, memorable time. But I'm not so sure we'll be invited back.

— *August 2008*

Patron Saints to Know and Love

It's that time of year again. Saint Valentine's Day is just around the corner, and Saint Patrick is headed over the horizon. No matter what your religious affiliation, if any, I'll bet these two saints give you cause for some sort of celebration.

We Catholics have a saint to celebrate every day of the year, a patron saint for just about any occasion. There's a heavenly host of them out there ready to help. All you need do is ask.

Saint Francis is well-known as the patron saint of animals. I send out a brief prayer for his assistance whenever I see a forlorn dog seeking adoption. I shouted a prayer to Saint Francis the afternoon I found my dear departed cat, Petunia, impaled on nail in a scrap heap. She lived many more happy years. I cried to Saint Francis the morning I scooped up a six-ounce kitten from the middle of Interstate 64. She is five years old now. Her name is ZuZu, and all 22 pounds of her is asleep on my bed at the moment.

One saint I turn to regularly is Saint Anthony, the patron saint of lost things; he's never let me down. Take, for instance, the beautiful gold earrings my mother bought me about 30 Christmases ago. I lost one in a hotel room at Virginia Beach. I tore the room apart, to no avail. I asked Saint Anthony to help me find it, but had to leave without the precious bauble. Well, I sighed to myself, Saint Anthony can't help us every time we ask.

Months later, preparing for another trip, I found the earring nestled in the crack of my suitcase. A couple years later, I lost that very earring again. Somewhat sheepishly, I prayed to Saint Anthony. 'I've lost that very same earring again,' I told him. 'Please help me find it.'

Months passed. Spring turned to fall, which turned to winter, which turned to spring. Workmen came by the house for a project. One knocked at the door. He held out a paint-splotched hand.

"Ma'am," he said, "I found this in the driveway."

There was my earring; somewhat flattened, but repairable. I'm sure the painter wondered why I burst into tears at the sight of a mashed gold earring, but Saint Anthony knew.

I also rely regularly on Saint John the Evangelist. He's the patron saint of writers, and has helped me countless times. Back when I was a harried reporter, I called on Saint John every Wednesday. I renewed our acquaintance this morning, when this column was past its deadline.

Did you know there's a patron saint for gardeners? Saint Hyacinth, wouldn't you know. Bakers who need a loaf of bread or batch of cookies to come out of the oven nicely might consider asking Saint Elizabeth of Hungary for assistance. Saint Cecelia, the patron saint of musicians, has helped me warble through many a wedding, funeral or stage performance. There's even a patron saint for dental problems: Saint Apollonia. Poor Saint Apollonia. In ancient Greece, she was accosted by Roman soldiers, who tore out all her teeth before they murdered her.

I like to call on obscure patron saints – ones that everybody isn't bothering all the time. I figure Saint Michael, Saint Jude – all the superstar saints – are busy, busy, busy. It stands to reason that other saints are sitting around bored but saintly, praying that someone will ask them for help.

One night in a far-off city, my mother and I were in a motel. We were due for surgery at 5:30 the next morning. We were anxious. We could not sleep. We tossed, we turned, we sighed.

"I wonder who's the patron saint of a good night's sleep," I called over to Mom.

"If you know, I wish you'd tell me," she answered.

I thought a moment and then it hit me like a bolt of lightning.

"It's the twelve apostles!" I cried.

"The twelve apostles? Why?"

"Because they were a-dozin'!"

— February 2000

My Thanksgiving Feast

It's that time of year again: Thanksgiving. It's time for folks to start asking, "Are you cooking dinner this year?"

It's time for me to shout, "No!"

Several years ago, when Mom was recuperating from knee surgery, it befell upon me to cook Thanksgiving dinner. It seemed simple enough. Any organized person could, with close attention to time management, easily pull off Thanksgiving dinner. I'm an organized time manager. Piece of cake, or so I thought.

To paraphrase Richard Nixon, I am not a cook. I've attempted two small dinner parties; by the time guests arrived, I was sweaty and swearing. I'm a restaurant girl, through and through.

I began my preparations at 1:30 that November afternoon, with a 6 p.m. deadline.

"Do the pie first," Mom instructed from her pillow-piled bed.

Studying the recipe, I calculated it would take 30 minutes. Sadly, I didn't allow time for scrubbing pumpkin off the walls and ceiling, after a frightful mishap with the can opener. At 3 p.m., the pie came out of the oven. Oddly, the crust had almost disappeared; what remained had the consistency of an eraser. I checked the box of just-bake-it crust I'd brought over from my own fridge; the expiration date was October 1995.

(My home refrigerator serves as a display case for potentially delightful foods, until they get tossed in the garbage. I should just stand over the trashcan and toss in $5 bills, sparing myself the drudgery of grocery shopping.)

Next, I plopped a plump turkey breast into the roasting pan and rummaged around for a meat thermometer. Grabbing a mysterious mercury-filled glass implement, I made several futile attempts to stab it into the unyielding, clammy fowl. Something was awry.

I trundled back to mom's bedroom, holding the thing aloft.

"I can't get this meat thermometer into the turkey."

"That's a candy thermometer," she replied.

"Won't it work anyway?"

"Your Aunt Louise tried that and, when she opened the oven door, it exploded in her face," she intoned. "They never did get out all the glass."

Another disaster avoided.

Time ticked away. It was 4:30, and my "goose" was about the only thing cooked.

On to the stuffing – old bread, celery, boiling water, an egg, a shriveled apple I scrounged from the fridge. By now, so many recipes were scattered on the counters, I was mistaking one for the other. Maybe, I thought as I stirred the glutinous glob, the egg was supposed to go into something else? The stuffing was a sodden mass, but I forged onward.

It was 5:30. Dinner was due in 30 minutes and there were still mashed potatoes, yams, cranberries and, oh geez, the table to set.

"Don't forget the gravy," Mom called from her bed.

"Forget the gravy!" I shouted.

Some women putter around the kitchen. I muttered, and slammed cabinets. I, the neatnik, sported an apron streaked with doughy globs, flour and pumpkin goo. It was time for a sip of sherry. Better yet, a tumbler of scotch. I decided to scratch the yams; who needs two kinds of potatoes, anyway? I was never so glad to see my sister than when she strolled in at 5:45, ready to don her bib and tucker. She surveyed the counter, filled with bowls, drifts of flour, eggshells. She saw the pumpkin streaks on the wall. She looked at the table, strewn with cookbooks and the brown, crustless pie. "Lovely table," she sniffed.

She read my splatter-splotched menu and checked the stove.

"Where are the yams?"

"We're having mashed."

"It's not Thanksgiving without yams."

"There they are; be my guest."

My sister, the professional chef, deftly sprinkled the yams with brown sugar and honey and popped them in the microwave. Why didn't I think of that? Though I've never cared for cranberry sauce, I learned to love it that day. It comes in a little can. It is served cold. I opened one end of the can I'd brought from home and, holding it over a crystal bowl, opened the other end. The gelatinous glop plopped into the bowl. That's when I noticed "Dec. 97" clearly stamped into the top. I covered it with a sprig of parsley.

At 7:15 dinner was finally served. I sensed my little family searching for something gracious to say. Finally, my sister spoke.

"Interesting."

They say that laughter is the best medicine, and we've never laughed so much over a dinner in all our lives. For that, we are truly thankful.

— November 2001

The Joy of Meals on Wheels

It was the most profoundly wonderful experience.

Last week, for the first time, I delivered Meals on Wheels.

It may have been the first time, but it won't be the last. Mark my words, I will be doing this until I can no longer drive, and must have them delivered to me.

I saw an ad in the local paper a few weeks ago, "Desperately seeking Meals on Wheels drivers for Healing Springs."

Well, I thought, I live in Healing Springs. Why can't I do it?

There's nothing much I do, on a regular basis, for anyone else. Since I'm no longer a reading tutor, what, I wonder, is my community service?

So I called Jane Lyle, who organizes the program, and volunteered.

What took me so long?

In case you've ever wondered about delivering Meals on Wheels, here's what it will cost you: One day a week, or even one day a month; you decide; about 10 miles worth of gasoline; about 30 minutes of your time.

Here's what you will receive: The grateful smiles of those for whom you may be the only human contact they receive that day; the satisfaction of delivering what perhaps could be their only hot meal of the day; a heady euphoria that lasts for days on end.

I picked up my load – five hot dishes, five "cold" bags – at 11 a.m. I did not ask about the contents, but assume the meal included meat, a hot vegetable, some bread, some milk, and maybe an apple or an orange. I hope there was some dessert in there, too.

At my very first stop, a frail old dear answered the door almost before I knocked. I quickly discovered that one doesn't just hand over the meal and skedaddle. These folks want to chat.

"Are you married?" she wanted to know.

"No."

"Well honey, you're missing out," she replied, grasping my hand with her own aged, delicate one. "I was married to a good man. He's been dead for 29 years, this coming September."

"I'm sorry."

"Yes," she said, "my Mama and my Daddy are gone, too."

And then she began to cry.

Faced with a lady perhaps 90 years old, still sad about the passing of her parents, I began to tear up myself.

We discovered that I went to school with her nieces. "They're both such good girls," she said. "They call and visit when they can, but they live far away. You're a good girl, too."

It's been quite awhile since anyone called me good, or for that matter, a girl.

I got back in my car, and glanced at the house. She had tottered to the window, and was peering out, waving. I burst into tears. This deed was a lot more emotional than I'd imagined.

At another house, the lady was tending her garden of fabulous flowers. She had some things to carry, so we walked back to the house together. She, too, was probably nearing 90.

When I told her my name, she said, "Oh yes. I sat across from you at the firehouse at Thanksgiving."

Why didn't I, at 40 years her junior, recall that?

There was a long-married couple at the final house. They were cute as could be, and ever so grateful. They urged, "Please come back and visit; we hardly see anyone any more."

I think I will.

On my way back, I thought, I've got to send Meals treasurer Louise Carpenter a donation. Why have I never thought about this wonderful program before? The fates saw to it that, as I ran into the post office five minutes later, there was Louise. I hugged and thanked her for the profound experience. She thanked me for the check, but believe me, the profound pleasure was all mine.

Please consider making it yours, too.

— April 2006

Christmas Spirit: A Special Delivery

Here's a story about a miracle of Christmas Past.

It began with a trip to the Christmas Mother Shop in Hot Springs.

I had "promised" – or so my mother implied – to help wrap presents that day. I *hate* wrapping, probably because I'm not very good at it. Once, I even managed to somehow tape together the fingers of my left hand. But the "elves" needed all the help they could get. Even if it was me.

As I raced out my door – already late – a huge wreath crashed to the porch, spewing bits of pine cone everywhere. I fumed, cursing all the blasted decorations. They were a bother; why did we need them, anyway?

Driving to the shop, I felt guilty about my outburst. I looked heavenward. "I'm begging you, Lord, give me some Christmas Spirit today!"

I stomped into the shop, a hint of a fake smile on my face. I stood by Mom and wrapped just one gift. Then she sweetly suggested I might want to run the wrapped gifts to the proper boxes. That was easier said than done. There were 120 giant boxes; more, in fact, since the gifts for some families had overflowed into three, even four boxes.

The "coming together" of the Christmas Mother Shop is a holiday miracle all its own.

Throughout the day, high school students trooped in and set to work wrapping and stuffing and bagging. Before you knew it, they were gone and another busload arrived. Anybody who bemoans the alienation of today's youth should stop by the shop and take a gander at reality. It could bring tears to your eyes.

In addition to mountains of gifts and toys, and the astounding amount of foodstuffs, there are clothes. Many are brand new; others nearly so. They fill five tables, four benches, countless boxes, and two 40-foot racks. I began folding the clothes on the tables, hanging the more fabulous things – cashmere sweaters, Ann Taylor blouses, Talbot skirts.

An old man in ragged clothes appeared at my elbow. All he really wanted was some socks. I found a pair of thick, soft wool.

"These will keep my feet real warm!"

I found another pair. When I tried to give him a third, he stopped me.

"I don't want to take too much," he said quietly.

"Don't you need anything else?"

"Well, I could use a coat."

We began to look. He was rangy, with long arms, and not too many things fit him. I found him a sport coat, and a pair of matching pants. Then we spotted a natty navy wool pin-stripe suit. It seemed just his size.

"This is real nice," he said. "I could wear this to church."

I asked, "Do you have a raincoat?"

"No."

"Well, you do now," I said, handing him a tan London Fog.

His eyes were bright. His smile was grand, despite a few missing teeth.

He needed shoes. And lo, we found a new pair of soft black shoes, just his size.

He hung his head. "This is too much," he said.

"Well, there's plenty. You'll do us a favor by taking it."

"I have two suits!" he happily exclaimed. "I don't guess you'd have a white shirt?"

The men's dress shirt selection was paltry. We had a couple with 17-inch collars, but he needed a 15 ½.

I had handled nearly every piece of clothing, and seen no other white shirts. Nonetheless, I went back to the tables, praying, "Dear Lord, please help me find a 15½ white shirt."

There it was: A white Christian Dior, size 15 ½. I looked up toward heaven and began to laugh.

"Seek, and you shall find!" I called out to the man.

As he left, with suits and shirt and shoes and raincoat and even a few items he could give as gifts, he shook my hand.

"You're an angel," he said. "God bless you for helping me."

The blessings were all mine. And so was the true Spirit of Christmas.

— December 2001

An Exciting Trip to the Dump

You've heard it before: One man's trash is another man's treasure.

The other day, I was showing some decorators around the Historical Society museum. I don't know why, but I kept pointing out things that "came from the dump."

We have one particular member who keeps a sharp eye out whenever she goes to the Dumpsters, and has shown up at our door with all kinds of treasures. And, as I've admitted in this column before, I am not averse to rescuing Dumpster treasures myself.

Thus, as I proudly held aloft a lovely old framed print, proclaiming "We found this at the dump, too!" the decorators observed, "Boy, you spend a lot of time at the dump."

Where did this dump fixation find its way into my psyche?

I certainly knew nothing of dumps in my earliest years. We lived in a city. Daddy took the trash to the curb. Early in the morning, noisy men in an even noisier truck picked it up and hauled it away somewhere. And that was that.

Then, we moved to the country. One day, I'd done some apparently horrendous deed, which caused my father to announce that all my dolls and doll clothes were "going to the dump."

And just like that, they disappeared.

"The dump" took on mystical, magical proportions to me.

I wanted to get to that dump and see it for myself. If my dolls and doll clothes could be found, imagine what other delights rested there. In my mind, "the dump" was a wonderland.

One exciting day, the opportunity arose.

I'm sure my parents had long forgotten the dolls-to-the-dump incident (turns out they were safely secured in a closet), but I had not. I wanted to get to that dump in the worst way.

"You girls want to ride to the dump?" Daddy inquired.

Did we ever.

Every Saturday, Daddy borrowed someone's pickup truck, and took our trash to what folks around here called "the crematory." That word, too, took on magical qualities; it sounded like a place where chocolate milk might be available.

So, Daddy loaded up our trash, and then my sister and I got into the back of the pickup truck along with it. Nowadays, that state trooper would be breaking law; back then, the backs of pickup trucks were simply where children rode.

It was my first such ride. And oh, how glorious it was. I grasped the back window tightly and the wind whipped my hair and it seemed as if we were sailing along at 100 miles an hour. No matter that I was surrounded by the garbage and detritus of everyday life; this was an exciting adventure!

We turned into the crematory, and the first thing we saw was a flat field of dirt with all sorts of fountains. When I inquired about this, Daddy explained the workings of a sewer system. Once I imagined that every time someone flushed a toilet, the fountains spewed, the place didn't seem so lovely, after all.

But then, there it was: The Dump!

In reality, it was not the wonderland I'd imagined. Hundreds of heaps of trash burned and smoked, giving the place a grayish haze. There were people there, poking through the piles with sticks. I saw no dolls, no doll clothes, no neat toys. The dump wasn't so alluring after all.

Daddy, too, had noticed the people poking through the piles. He saw some of the same families there every week. And that gave him an idea.

Kids outgrow toys all the time. So, it came to pass that when we outgrew our toys, they would disappear into Daddy's furnace-room workshop. My father was always an artist at heart. He took those toys and made them better than new. And then he took them to the dump on a Saturday, and carefully placed them nowhere near a burning trash heap. They never stayed there long.

— February 2003

The Big Ugly

"There's nothing like a cancer scare to help put your life in perspective."

I planned to write that sentence, as soon as I found out I had nothing to worry about. Now, I have lots to worry about. And "scare" becomes the operative word.

If I were a bird, I'd be an ostrich. Flamboyant. Territorial. And prone to hiding its head in the sand.

This week, I am forced to pull my head out of the sand and face facts: I have cancer.

People in the know keep telling me not to get overly worried. That's easy for them to say.

Two weeks ago, after my big move, I hopped in the car and went adventuring through West Virginia, which truly is wild and wonderful. I went whitewater rafting. I read three books. Nobody knew my name. A very successful vacation.

I discovered Hawk's Nest State Park, near Ansted, W.Va. As I donned my bathing suit for a bout of poolside reading, I made another discovery. It was heart-stopping.

I'm certainly not in the habit of looking at my backside, but I happened to catch sight of it in the mirror that afternoon. There it was: A big, black, ugly blotch, in the center of my back — that place you never can quite reach to scratch.

I looked in the phone book for a dermatologist; the nearest doctor of any sort was in Charleston. It was Wednesday; with Labor Day looming, it would be Tuesday before I could see Dr. Redington and Barbara Howell (back home).

The last few days of vacation were far from relaxing. Amid nature's glory, where nobody knew my name, I contemplated mortality.

By Tuesday morning, I had roiled up quite an anxiety. After 10 minutes in the doctor's office, things really shifted into higher gear.

"Just to be on the safe side," I'd have to see a specialist in Roanoke. But fortune smiled; that very doctor, plastic surgeon Michael Breiner, was due at Bath Community Hospital in 30 minutes.

Thank heavens for BCH, the comfy, friendly little hospital we are so fortunate to have. While waiting for Dr. Breiner, I laughed and cried with nurses Becky and Collie, old school pals. The doctor arrived and, almost before I knew it, did a biopsy. Learning the results could take another five days.

But not at BCH. Becky hand-carried the little piece of horror down to Alleghany; Dr. Breiner leaned on his pathology colleagues; by lunchtime Wednesday, I heard the words I'd hoped not to hear: Malignant melanoma.

It was time to tell my family. There are just the three of us now; Daddy died from cancer in 1990.

My mother and sister took my news well. There were no tears. In fact, true to quirky family form, we found ourselves laughing uproariously.

As soon as I broke the news, Mom and Kathy leapt from their seats. 'Time for a group hug,' I thought. But no. They pantomimed elbowing each other out of the way as they raced toward my new addition to Mom's house, "arguing" about who was going to claim which treasures first. Kathy suggested I do my Christmas shopping early. Mom mused aloud about my life insurance, and tropical vacations.

Laughing in the face of adversity sure beats wallowing in woe.

I'm determined to be positive: I may lose weight. I will quit smoking. I can march in the Survivor's Walk at the Relay for Life. I just might become a nicer person.

The situation abounds with irony and little blessings: Had I not discovered "it" when I did, I would not have been in a bathing suit until next summer. Or probably ever, according to Dr. Breiner, who emphasized that early detection had "saved my life." If I'd found a West Virginia dermatologist, I'd have been at the mercy of medical strangers, rarely the least bit comforting. By waiting almost a week, I'm being cared for by friends and professionals I trust.

And then there's Dr. Breiner. Due at BCH in 30 minutes, for his once-a-month mission? Blessed coincidence. After the biopsy, he took my hand and said, "All we can do now is pray. And I want you to know that I pray for my patients every night."

When was the last time a physician told you that?

So, at 11:30 a.m. today, Friday, Sept. 17, I'll be drifting into dreamland at Lewis Gale Hospital. Dr. Breiner will slice what sounds like a startlingly large piece of skin from my back, and then "sew it up real pretty."

I wish he'd throw in some liposuction and maybe a chin job, but I guess that's too much to ask.

After surgery, he says, "We'll wait for results, and pray for the best." Amen.

— September 1999

My Lucky Day

How could a day I faced with great dread turn into such a good time?

I tried to keep it as quiet as possible, telling only my closest friends that melanoma might be rearing its ugly, insidious head again.

One pal offered to drive me to the surgical oncologist in Charlottesville this week. That was a superb favor. I couldn't sleep the night before the appointment. And although I woke feeling determined and mustering courage, I had a panic attack first thing.

Thank heavens I still have a few anti-anxiety pills on hand from my last ordeal. They're almost five years old now, but I found a piece of one crumbling in the bottom of my purse, and felt no compunction at all about tossing it down my throat.

Back in January, I started thinking how, come September, I could mark five years of being cancer-free. Then things seemed to unravel. I shook my head at the irony of it all – now, just three months short of the anniversary I planned to celebrate, I might be thrust into the vortex again.

The first thing I really, really didn't want to do was go back to the waiting room at the cancer center. I have an aversion to Charlottesville in general. I spent four months traipsing back and forth there when my father was dying. I spent two months being driven back and forth when I was sick. I'd come to detest the town.

And the oncologist's waiting room on the fourth floor is hands-down the saddest place I've ever been. I'll say this: If you're feeling rather sorry for yourself, just spend a few minutes there, and you'll snap right out of it.

My friend and I spent far more than a few minutes there Monday. My appointment was at noon. We arrived at 11:30. Things seemed to be hustling right along, and then came to an abrupt halt. Those of us packed into the room put up a good pretense of reading, but our eyes would seek out one another. We knew what we, or our accompanying family member, faced. With just a glance, we'd communicate empathy, sympathy, and best wishes.

The room was filled, yet almost no one talked about disease. And if they did, it was in a positive way. One woman, in a wheelchair and bald from chemotherapy, was asked about her jaunty pink-flowered hat. "Oh, it was just the most fun thing," she said. "All my friends got together for my birthday. Each one wore this hat in a different color – yellow, blue, green – and then they all gave me their hats as a present. I have one to match every outfit," she proudly declared.

God bless her. May she have many more birthdays.

I try not to think about the pretty young woman who was crying out loud when she left the doctor's office with her parents. "We'll go see another doctor right away," her mother vowed.

Time ticked past as we sat there. Then I overheard a woman mention her appointment was at 10 o'clock. I checked my watch; it was 1 p.m. I asked the receptionist about the delay. "Oh," she smiled, "he's running about two hours behind."

We decided to leave for lunch, and my friend mentioned a Cuban restaurant downtown. There was nothing that could have made me more excited.

We sat at a table outside. I wolfed down the best Cuban sandwich this side of Key West. I felt much, much better.

When we returned to the waiting room, we were actually giggling. There was a sort of party atmosphere about the place. At 3:10 p.m., they called my name. By 4:10 p.m., I learned I probably don't have anything to worry about. I skipped back to the waiting room. Most every eye looked at me, and when I smiled with relief, they smiled, too. I hope it boosted their courage; good news can happen, even in that sad place.

— June 2004

The Turtle Takes the Prize

I never liked Halloween as a child. First, there was the pressure of dreaming up and then creating a costume. The dreaming up was not so much a problem as the execution. I always wanted to be, say, a dance-hall girl, and my mother always thought a hobo or a clown was more appropriate.

There's a two-part photo of me in costume at age four. Part One shows a sweet little girl in a black velvet evening gown and pearls. Part Two shows the back view: Me in underpants and sturdy brown oxfords. The "dress" was just a façade.

I chuckle over those photos. They capture what is even today "the real me" – putting up a good front, but don't look too closely.

I barely recall the hoboes and clowns of my youth. My best Halloween costume ever came at age 25, in Key West.

I must note here that Key West is a town that knows how to throw a Halloween party. Every day of the year, truth be told.

I was working at Treasure Salvors, spending lots of time at sea, and hanging out with a crew of Adonis-like divers. As Halloween approached, I pondered my costume for the big party at The Monster – the best bar in town, favored watering hole of fellows with a proclivity for wearing evening gowns, Halloween or not.

One of the divers had a turtle shell on his wall; a trophy, if you will, of some lawless undersea deed. I stared at it one night, and knew immediately: I would be a turtle.

Using straps from an old dive tank, we fashioned the turtle shell – about two feet in diameter – into a sort of backpack. I wore a green leotard, green tights, and shiny key-lime green patent-leather clogs. Yes, these were items in my everyday closet at that time.

The real poser was headgear, to carry off the turtle theme. I bought some green and some yellow felt, and set to work. I made a green hood, and cut out some eye holes. Then came a yellow beak, the most important feature of any turtle costume. I bent part of a coat hanger into a V-shape, and attached that to the hood.

Did I mention that I'm hastily working on this hood because my friends are due to arrive at any moment to go to the party? My life is a series of last-minute creative scurries.

I scrabbled through the kitchen drawer, looking for something to attach the yellow felt to the beak. I found some model airplane glue and set to work. My creation was completed the very minute the doorbell rang.

My friends strapped me into the big, heavy shell. I affixed the beaked hood to my head and we set off, on our bicycles, toward The Monster.

We pedaled through the chilly night, down Simonton Street, across Greene, and toward Duval. I was huffing and puffing under the warm hood. We breezed past Sloppy Joe's, the usual crowd gathered on the sidewalk.

"Hey! Look at the turtle!" some reveler shouted. People clapped, as best they could, holding plastic cups of cheap beer.

I thought it was extremely funny. In fact, I felt extremely funny. Turns out, the airplane glue I'd used to affix the beak had not had time to dry. With every breath I took I was, well, sniffing glue.

By the time we reached The Monster, I was giddy as all get out. I had absolutely the best Halloween party-time of my life. I danced with wild abandon among gaggles of men dressed as an entire wedding party – replete with 250-pound bridesmaids in pink chiffon – plus Judy Garland, Snow White with seven scantily-attired dwarves, and myriad other characters I shan't mention here.

I won first prize.

— October 2001

Two Empty Chairs

I learned a heartbreaking, heartwarming lesson about rural living recently.

My darling mother passed away rather suddenly September 15. Although my sister and I were in the process of preparing ourselves for this eventuality, we were taken by surprise. Mom had been hospitalized for "a day or two" to be treated for dehydration. She looked great Wednesday afternoon. Thursday morning at 5:15, they called to tell us she was gone.

As these things happen, it was, I guess, a lovely way to go.

Mom had spent her last day at home that Monday, sitting on a bench in my sister's glorious flower garden. The sun warmed her face. Butterflies fluttered about, and the birds she loved were singing. My sister Kathy kept an eye on the window as she bustled about, cleaning the house.

But then, Kathy looked out and saw the bench was empty. Mom, who had suffered a series of countless "small" strokes, was not one to wander. Then, my sister noticed something disturbing – two little white sneakers, poking up from under the Rose of Sharon bush.

We figured Mom had fallen asleep and pitched off the bench into the bush. The rescue squad was called.

When I got to the emergency room, my mother looked quite ghastly. Tests showed severe dehydration. She'd have to be admitted for a night or two.

Tuesday, she looked much better. By Wednesday, she was sitting in a chair, smiling that dear, sweet smile, and chatting with my friend and me.

"I'm going home tomorrow," she told us confidently.

Driving back to the house, I told my friend, "There's no way she's going home tomorrow; she can't even walk!"

What did I know?

Mom went home, indeed. And now she can fly.

As soon as the pre-dawn call from a curt and unsympathetic hospital worker came, my life took a sad new turn. But that's also when I learned even more about the wonders of rural living.

I learned I didn't have to make but, say, four calls before the news had spread across the county and beyond. I learned that I'd better spiff up the house by 6:30 a.m., because callers would be coming by with brownies, deli platters, flowers, paper products and still-warm lasagnas. I learned that going to the post office can be comforting; rather than a sheaf of bills, the box is crammed with condolence cards.

I learned that the visitation at the funeral home can be a wonderful, consoling thing, characterized more by laughter than tears. I learned that hundreds of people from all walks of life loved my mother almost as much as I did.

Despite the fact that I broke out in hives the night before, Mom's funeral turned out to be the most lovely, uplifting experience of my life.

At the cemetery, I learned that, despite my sorrow, I could indeed sing, a capella, the Latin hymn "In Paradisum." I also learned that, even if a bee landed on my lips during the song, I could keep on singing. I'm convinced my mother's hand, no longer gnarled by arthritis, brushed it away. I guess she's no longer afraid of bees, either.

Now the holidays are upon us. My sister and I will have to learn how to celebrate November 19, Mom's birthday, without the guest of honor. We will have a small, and probably sad, Thanksgiving. We will, I know, give thanks for our loving parents, and be comforted by the belief that they are together again, forever.

There will now be two empty chairs at the Thanksgiving table. Getting used to Daddy's empty chair took years. I can't imagine we'll ever adjust to Mom's chair being vacant, too.

There will now be two empty chairs around the Christmas tree, and the gleeful laughter that always accompanied the opening of presents will, I guess, be impossible to recapture. This year, there won't be a silly picture of Mom with a red bow on her forehead. She won't be sitting in the pew at midnight Mass. There really won't be much "Joy to the World" in our hearts.

We should probably consider whisking ourselves to some tropical, almost alien locale, for the holidays. Someplace that wouldn't be rife with memories.

But no. We owe a debt of gratitude, and loving heap of honor, to those empty chairs.

— September 2005

Original publication dates

The following were first published in The Virginian Review, Covington:

Of Knives and Pantyhose: January 2004
Dominus Vobiscum: May 2010
My Parochial Revenge: April 2007
Daddy Grabs a Bomb: October 2006
Daddy's Parting Gift: July 2001
Just a Little Fire: April 2001
Flying Miss Daisy: December 2002
Alarming Trip to the Big City: September 2000
Revenge of the Critters: June 2009
The Critters Have their Say: June 2009
No Bother at All: July 2003
Snooping with Dogs: March 2003
Like Cats and Dogs: December 2006
A Toddler in the House: March 2009
I Encounter a Vicious Beast: February 2002
Max's Curious Adventure: June 2005
Swimming with the Fishes: July 2001
Dallying with the Dolphins: June 2002
Say Hay!: April 2005
Bee Very Afraid: May 2002
Whistle While You Work: June 2005
The Mystery of the Missing Nuggets: January 2005
I Learn to Play Ball: October 2004
Jailbirds: May 2001
The Mishappetizer: November 2003
A Yacht in the Aegean: August 2004
Something in Common, After All: February 2009
I Venture to Havana: May 2002
I am Handy!: October 2008
Somebody Laves Me: July 2003
I Learn New Tricks: July 2006

The Party Dog: August 2008
Patron Saints to Know and Love: February 2000
The Joy of Meals on Wheels: April 2006
Christmas Spirit: A Special Delivery: December 2001
An Exciting Trip to the Dump: February 2003
My Lucky Day: June 2004
The Turtle Takes the Prize: October 2001

**The following were first published in
Cooperative Living magazine:**

We're on the Right Road!: June 2010
Babies, Boomer and Rutabaga: September 2002
Of Pasta and Panic: May 2003
Ask Auntie Margo: August 2004
The Dreaded Drone of Danger: July 2005
Wherein I Ride an Elephant: February 2003
Regrets: I Have a Few: July 2008
A Letter from my Contractor: October 2008
Selling Country Property: August 2006
Those Were the Days My Friend, We Thought They'd Never End: August 2009
June: National Rural Laundry Month: June 2008
The Kinky Burglar: December 2006
In Praise of Pillows: August 2009
My Favorite Sentence: February 2002
Love a Teacher: Rural Teachers: August 2011
Shattered Expectations: April 2007
An Unhappy Camper: April 2009
I Love to Snovel Show: February 2007
The Pokey Dokes: May 2004
The Rural Wave: July 2007
On the Rivah: October 2006
The Surprise Wedding: August 2004
My Thanksgiving Feast: November 2001
Two Empty Chairs: September 2005

The following was first published in The Recorder:
The Big Ugly: September 1999